FREEING
FARIDA

FREEDOM IS A DESTINATION FOR THE SOUL

DOTUN DAWODU

13TH & JOAN

For permission requests, write to the publisher, addressed "Attention: Permissions Coordinator," 205 N. Michigan Avenue, Suite #810, Chicago, IL 60601. 13th & Joan books may be purchased for educational, business or sales promotional use. For information, please email the Sales Department at sales@13thandjoan.com.

Printed in the U. S. A.

First Printing, July 2022.

Library of Congress Cataloging-in-Publication Data has been applied for.

ISBN: 978-1-953156-11-2

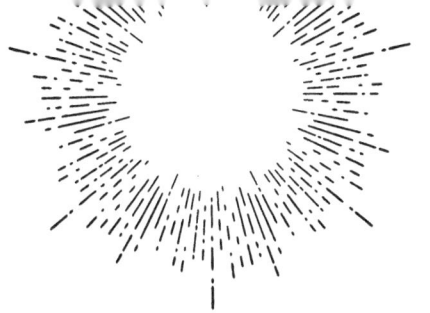

DEDICATION

I dedicate Freeing Farida to
"ALL MY CHILDREN & GRANDCHILDREN"
both biological and non-biological.

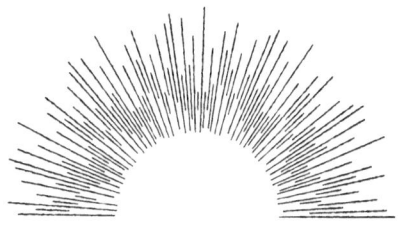

EPIGRAPH

"When the still small voice speaks, think and act"
— Dotun Dawodu

"One does not have time, only opportunity."
— Ade Ademola.

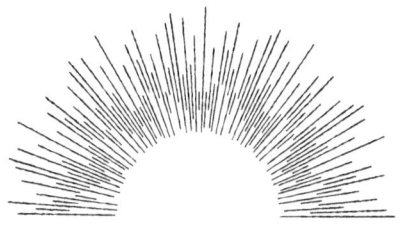

FOREWORD

"YOU WILL NOT reap over any of them. You have labored over them, all of your labor will not be in vain, my darling Elena." As a single mom of five children, these words sent to me via text by Mama held such a deep space in my heart. They felt as if I had been given a big hug that released all doubt about me raising my children as a single parent for the last 13 years. This was just one of the many texts she sent me over the years to give me encouragement, comfort, and love.

When I met "Mama" many years ago, I instantly felt as if our souls had met before. Our stories were somehow intertwined. She'd lived before me and shared this incredible energy that gave me so much comfort and confidence as I was embarking on the latter years of motherhood. I would often think of all the mothers out there. If they could just share half of what I felt when I read her messages, then they too would have been given hope and encouragement that empowered them to continue to move forward.

This is what *Freeing Farida* is. It's her story, the very essence of who she is, the lessons, love, encouragement, fun, and hope that she has given in doses over the years and now sharing with the world. On any continent, in any language, this will be a must-read.

Your Spiritual Daughter,
Elena Taylor

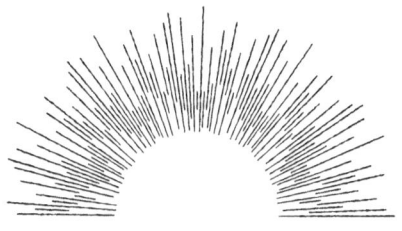

PREFACE

If I had to do it again, I would without hesitation.

TODAY, I AM happy to report Farida is doing very well. She is happily married and has three beautiful children. She has a wonderful career doing what she loves and life is great for her in many ways. This was not always the case. I remember the day I rescued Farida from Didi like it was yesterday. My morning routine consists of waking up with my thank you's for life, prayer, and devotion, and looking at the sky. If weather permits, I take a walk and enjoy the beauty of the sky. This practice has forever changed my life. I get lost in the marvelous colors and weather patterns. Each day I am in awe of the wonders of GOD.

This particular morning, as I was looking at the sky, I heard a voice say, "Go take her away from where she is being abused." I heard the voice and did not question it, I instantly knew it was from GOD. This voice was so significant and clear, that I knew I *had* to obey it.

I was the person the assignment was given to and I had to act and act fast. There was no time to think of anything but rescuing her. I could not think of breakfast or the next moment. The only thing on my mind that morning was getting Farida out of there. I had been hearing stories of how Farida was being treated poorly and abused, however, no one was doing anything about it. It was not unusual for me to get a phone call with the news of the day of how Farida was being treated. I would hear stories of her being beaten, starved, abused, and locked up. It was shocking to me that someone could treat another human being this way. I would hang up the phone, I would pray for her and I thought of her often throughout the day. However, I had no idea at the time I would be the person brave enough to rescue her.

When the voice came to me, I had no idea where Farida was living nor did I know the plan of how I was going to rescue her. The details certainly were not clear to me and I had no direction whatsoever, the only direction I had was knowing GOD would be with me. Long after the mission was accomplished, my brother was upset with me because he feared I was putting my life in danger. I understood the concerns and did not take the time to take any of them into consideration. After pleading with my sister, she decided to help me in the right direction and gave me Lulu's phone number for assistance and information for rescuing Farida. Immediately, the plan went into motion. This book will reveal the story of how I freed Farida from Didi. If I had to do it again, I would without hesitation.

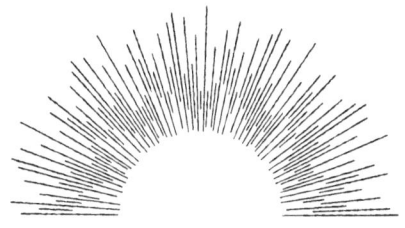

ACKNOWLEDGMENTS

I WOULD LIKE TO thank Tara (Sunshine) and Toni, (Little Miracle) my darling granddaughters who made the writing of Freeing Farida come to pass.

Tara donated her bone marrow so Toni could live! Our little Miracle was born with sickle cell disease. As Toni's primary Caregiver after her hospitalization, I had to get busy when she was always engaged, making bracelets to donate to sick children to forget the pain she was going through ~ thus the birth of Freeing Farida. I love you both Sunshine and Miracle.

I would like to thank my Father (deceased) and Mother, for the strength they instilled in me. I'm strong because strong parents birthed me. Thank you Papa mi and Sister mi (as we fondly call our Mom). I love you and always will.

I thank my siblings.

- Bola (My Aunt who grew up with us)
- Sina (Deceased)
- Dayo
- Yewande (Deceased)
- Tolu
- Kemi

Love was and is still our language. The love we shared as children living under the same roof and still share across the globe also made freeing Farida possible. We laughed together , cried together, got into trouble together and played together as children and we enjoyed every minute of those days. The sweet memories of our childhood will remain with me until I take my last breath. Unforgettable and precious they were. I love you all.

Akin and Funke, my children from other parents, I thank you both for always being there for me day in and night out during the writing of Freeing Farida. Always asking me how far I had gone with the writing. Now I can rest.

I am free from being questioned.

Freeing Farida is completed.

I love you both.

Beautiful Ardre and Precious Shakira, on making Freeing Farida possible, I appreciate you both for all you have done. You're simply wonderful and I thank you from the bottom of my heart. Looking forward to working with you and 13th and Joan for many books to come. I love you.

Thank you my dear friend Dee for your love, care, and support during my trying period in London. An interesting section of Freeing Farida wouldn't have been penned if you didn't intervene during those difficult days. You're greatly appreciated and I love you.

I would like to acknowledge Oliver Enwonwu and Olasehinde Odimayo. Thank you very much for the beautiful cover page.

Idunnu and Eniayo, my wonderful daughters, precious jewels, and beautiful angels, I thank you both for everything!!! We have been through the good, the bad, and the ugly together. For not judging me about the bad and the ugly journey, I thank you!!! I thank you so much for your contribution to the title "Freeing Farida." Farida came from Eniayo and Idunnu added the Freeing which gave the true meaning of the story. I love you both very very much.

I also want to thank all my extended family, spiritual children, and friends, who have been a positive part of my life. I appreciate and love you all.

The Lord bless you all.

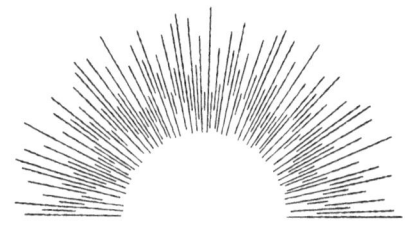

TABLE OF CONTENTS

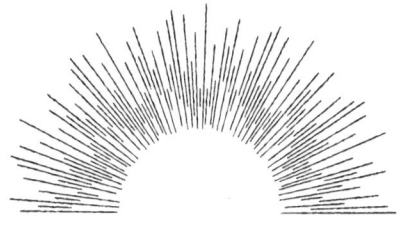

INTRODUCTION

I AM NOT WRITING this book for fame or fortune. I am not writing this book to be considered some sort of hero. I am writing this book to tell the story of how I rescued a young lady named Farida. I feel it is time for the story to be told. There may be a trafficked victim right under your nose and if so, I pray after reading this book, you help them. This story will serve as a guide to heed that inner voice when it comes to you with information and instructions. If you listen to the voice and obey, you will be fulfilled. The voice will never be wrong or provide incorrect instructions. Looking back on that time of my life, I am glad I answered the voice and am also grateful the voice came to me. Many people heard Farida's story and did not do anything about it. Instead of trying to help her, the situation became a subject of gossip and "let me tell you what has happened to her today." I wonder how it would have turned out had I not listened to the voice. Would she still be involved with the Didi as a human trafficking victim? Would she still be alive today? Would she have eventually escaped on her own? Where would she be today? Would someone else eventually have saved her? So many questions, thankfully, these questions do not need to be answered. Farida has been freed.

You are not scared in this situation. The voice spoke in a way that erased all fear. I was given the courage to succeed at the mission of saving someone in deep trouble. Had I not listened and something negative happened to Farida, (who had tried to take her own life before I stepped in), I would have been as guilty as her employer. I would have been guilty because I heard the voice and did nothing. I wasn't scared because I believed it was a mission I had to do. Because I am a believer in the Spirit of the Almighty and my beliefs made it very easy for me to proceed. My brother was so angry with me for getting involved in rescuing Farida. I was trying to take care of a situation no one else wanted to take care of. Farida worked with Didi for three years. Didi's friends and family knew and saw what was going on and did not know what to do. Nonetheless, I was sent to do it. Today, Farida has a fulfilling life and she is very happy. During the media press conference years ago, I was bombarded with questions. One of the policemen asked me if I was scared to do it and I told him "NO". He asked if I would do it again and I told him if I am sent to do it, I would. Today, I am glad I listened and more glad I obeyed. When GOD sends you a direct message, he gives you the courage to prepare for it. It is when we do things in the flesh, that we make mistakes. I'm talking from experience because when we act in the flesh, we do not think about consequences. Sometimes our missions are successful and sometimes not. When it is the voice of GOD, it will be successful.

It is a spiritual experience that cannot be explained. I listened to the story of this poor girl for months. I would listen and not think of doing anything about the information I heard. The particular morning I heard the voice, I heard it was meditating and thinking of the awesomeness of the Almighty. The "voice" speaks to us all and it is when we listen and hear it, that we are connected to HIM. I was divinely connected through nature. If I was anywhere else,

I would not have heard it because my mind would have been somewhere else. At that moment, I was thinking about my Creator, my Almighty Father. Each time I heard about Farida, I would feel sorry for her and my prayer was that one day, she would be free. I didn't hear the voice the day before or weeks before. When I heard the voice, within an hour I was out of the house and the mission to rescue her, by His grace, was successful.

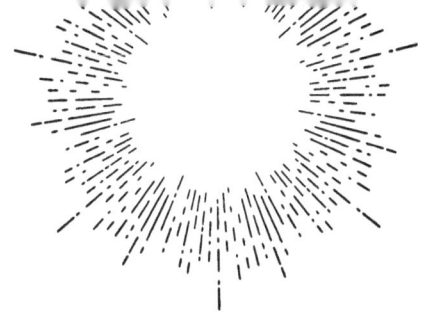

CHAPTER ONE:
ASUNDER

The brightest light shines amidst the darkest hours.

I GREW UP A shy, introverted girl in Nigeria. Only interested in getting good grades and a good career when I graduated, I could spend hours with my nose in a book.

When I was young, I had a crew of four best friends that I'd known since we were little. We did everything together. We would walk to and from school together and frequently had sleepovers at each other's houses at weekends. They were the best girlfriends you could have asked for, authentic and genuine. I could be myself around them.

I kept pace with Dee and Temi as we walked along the path back home. Of the four girls, Dee and Temi were closest to me. They were the ying to my yang, sassy and outspoken like firecrackers. I loved them like we were sisters and as we had gotten older, we were always there for each other during heartbreaks.

I was still reeling from the breakup with my ex-boyfriend just last week. He had cheated on me with a girl who despised me. A girl who had pushed my books out of my hands in class and generally tormented me whenever she had the opportunity to do so. She was a real menace.

I cried on my best friends' shoulders for hours. Of all our classmates, he had cheated on me with *her*. I kept my eyes forward, stuffing down the heartache, determined to soldier through.

"I can't stand basketball boys," Temi said, loud enough for us to hear. "They're all a bunch of downright naughty boys. Every single one of them cheats."

I didn't want anything to do with them or any boy for that matter. With the weekend fast approaching, I wanted to get out of the house and hang out with my girlfriends before my mother made plans for me.

"Why don't we throw a party this weekend?" Dee chimed in, turning the conversation away.

I heard the thud of the basketball before I saw them, turning up to squint against the sunlight at the group of boys walking towards us. They huddled together, casting quick glances in our direction while whispering amongst themselves.

I felt my face get hot, as the distance between our two groups closed. I didn't notice him at first, not until he crossed my path and nearly broke his neck as he did a double-take, looking at *me*.

My cheeks exploded in flame, he was looking at me? Me, in my oversized dress, with cornrows in my hair. Damn, I should've made sure my hair looked good when I left this morning.

"Hey Sola," he called. "Where are you going right now?"

I stopped as did my friends, turning to look behind me. Temi linked her arm through mine quickly.

"She's not going anywhere with you." Her neck rolled as she snapped back at him.

"Why don't you let Sola speak for herself?" One of his friends said.

Everyone turned to stare at me and for a moment everything went quiet. Everyone knew who Toks was. He was the star forward of our high school basketball team, the Scooters, and never scored less than thirty points a game. Six foot four with beautiful dark skin that glistened in the sunlight, every girl in school wanted to be on Toks' arm.

His family lived in a huge white mansion, the most beautiful building at the top of the hill near the city government offices. He came from an upper-middle-class home. His mother was a homemaker and his father was a doctor. They had every mother who knew their family lining their daughters up outside the door to marry one of their sons.

Toks spun the basketball in his hands, flashing me a perfect, white smile from beneath the shadow of his cap. He was handsome, my heart fluttering in my chest as I met his eyes. Out of all us girls, *I* was the one he stopped to talk to.

I didn't know how long I had been standing there, a goofy smile plastered on my face just staring at him before one of my friends answered for me.

"We're headed to Sola's house to do our homework. Where are you boys headed?"

"Do you want to walk with me, Sola?" he asked.

"Sure." I blurted, the word coming out of my mouth before I even thought to ask him where.

Temi sighed as I slipped away from her. "Don't do anything I wouldn't do." She called, hands on her hips and a frown pinched between her brows.

Everyone stared at us as we walked away. I ignored the chatter and tried not to look too eager as we headed away from my house and towards the park.

Toks swept me off my feet. We talked for hours, walking around the park for so long that I lost track of time. Flowers bloomed along the path in a myriad of colors so bright it felt like we stepped out of a scene in a romantic movie.

That evening, he took me out to dinner and ice cream, offering a scoop on his spoon for me to try, wiping the corner of my mouth with his thumb. My heart raced, a mix of embarrassment at the mess I was making and pure, unfettered puppy love.

Everything else faded away. Everything was all gone from my head, my homework, home, my ex-boyfriend, everything I should be thinking about at that time. All I wanted to do was spend more time with him. Toks was a classic example of "don't judge a book by its cover" At first,

I had assumed he was a playboy and a heartbreaker like all the rumors I'd heard about the boys on the basketball team, but Toks was in fact smart and genuine.

He wanted to get to know the real me and we discovered a mutual love for art, music and culture, like Maya Angelou, Fela Ransome Kuti, Ben Enwonwu, and Toni Morrison. Toks was the perfect gentleman.

We became the campus new "it" couple. He would meet me at my locker and hold my books as he walked me to class. He would buy me lunch and walk me home when he didn't have practice or a game.

When he did have a game, I was there front and center with my friends cheering him on. There was a time when the entire gym erupted with cheers and shouts as Toks sank the game-winning shot into the basket, turning to me with a smile and a wink.

We would talk the evenings away after school before I had to run home, just barely making it back before curfew.I wanted to spend every moment possible with Toks. And like every other mother, who wanted the best for her daughter, when my mother found out I was dating a son from the Abioye family, she was quick to give her blessing.

My parents worked incredibly hard to provide for our family and had high standards for what they required in someone who wanted to be with their daughters. Our families welcomed each other with open arms and in time we would become one big, happy family.

From that first day, Toks and I were inseparable. On my 23rd birthday, I held Toks' hand as we walked into Lagoon Restaurant in Victoria Island. As I stepped inside, the room erupted into exclamations.

"Happy birthday!" A chorus of cheers came.

Balloons scattered the room, candles flickering on the tables, and all of my friends and family waiting for me with open arms. It was the most magical evening.

Toks held me in his arms as we swayed to the music. He took my hands, flashing me that kilowatt smile before taking a step back and getting down on one knee. My heart raced, glancing around the room to see everyone standing around us in a circle holding their breath for what came next.

He pulled the princess cut diamond out from his pocket. I recognized it from months ago when Toks and I went shopping and stopped at the jewelry store. Tears streaming down my face, I managed to say "yes" and he slipped the ring on my finger. I was completely in love with Toks and wanted nothing more than to be with him until the end.

I'll never forget the look on his face as I approached him down the aisle. Overcome with emotion, tears swelling in his eyes, and that kilowatt smile looking only at me. If you would have asked me then, "Would we be together forever?" I would have answered with a steady yes. I would've yelled it from the rooftops and meant it with all of my heart.

When I found out I was pregnant for the first time, I was swept away in happiness. Many times he ran out at all hours of the night to get me *suya* and *akara* from my favorite restaurant. Toks never left my side, attending to my every need and even cutting the umbilical cord when my oldest daughter was born.

At last, we had our own little family and life reached a pinnacle of joy like never before. My dreams were coming true before my very eyes.

I always thought Toks and I had a great marriage. We were always able to communicate effectively and make amends when needed. We argued like any other married couple, but it never escalated past that, we worked it out together every step of the way.

When we walked down the street, people stopped us to marvel at how lovely our family was and always complimented our daughters Toke and Tori at every turn. They were beautiful girls, always dressed in fluffy, picturesque dresses and MaryJane shoes, ribbons bouncing in their pigtails.

They were both daddy's girls, and he doted on them at every turn. Since the beginning of our relationship back in high school, we talked about how we wanted our children to be well-rounded, and have the best in life, much greater than we had growing up. We wanted our children in the best schools with the best opportunities. We had a friendly, caring and supportive church home. This was non-negotiable for our marriage and we both worked hard to make it so. We loved our daughters, and we tried to give them the best at every opportunity.

Things were not perfect but our marriage worked for us, and together we were building a good future for our little girls. Our dream was to move from Nigeria to London. London had a booming Nigerian community and the job market was great. Toks finished his education and became an engineer. With that, he was able to find a well-paying job in London. We packed up our family and our lives and flew thousands of miles from everything we'd known to build a new life.

We had a beautiful Hampstead apartment with lush greenery surrounding the yard and the streets around our home. The girls could play outside safely and the neighborhood welcomed us with open arms.

We lived in a sprawling four-bedroom apartment and I poured my energy into creating a home for us. I filled it with antiques and unique African art pieces. I had African statues, paintings, beads, rugs, and pottery. You name it and I collected it over the years. Everything was hand-picked to perfection.

Our girls flourished at the local daycare. They made a lot of lovely friends and had amazingly attentive teachers. I joined the parent association and became very good friends with some of the other parents there.

I felt blessed to have a wonderful community of people who were there for each other. We had book clubs, play dates, and mom dinner dates. I was easing into a beautiful life as a wife and mother and enjoyed every minute of it. It was more than I could ever dream of, but something was starting to change within Toks.

Although Toks and I always had great communication, lately when we disagreed, it would turn into an all-out war. We'd always been good at mending fences and coming to common ground peacefully and respectfully. Suddenly, our arguments turned into screaming matches and I could see the dark cloud brewing over his head.

He came home every night disgusted and miserable, ranting and raving about the latest happenings at his job. He started complaining that he hated his career, the people he worked with, most notably his boss.

I was completely thrown off-guard. Toks had always been the type of man that made great decisions for himself and did not settle for less. If he didn't like the job he was on, he would change it and find something more accommodating.

He had started drinking more alcohol as the days wore on, furthering the rift in our family. Toks was cruel and heartless when he was drunk. He said whatever came to his mind, blaming me for his career troubles and his discontentment.

Every day it became more and more unbearable to be near him. He wasn't happy anymore, with us or himself. I spent more time watching tv by myself in the family room after the girls went to bed.

There was a time when Toks screamed from across the apartment, hurling words mixed together from the drink.

Tears welled in my eyes as Toke grabbed my hand and asked, "Mommy, is daddy okay?"

Things had changed for the worst. I thought I had it all. It was like the veil was ripped from my eyes and I finally saw the truth. My marriage was failing right before my eyes. We'd become distant from one another. I was with the girls more than normal and he was not happy anymore which permeated everything. His attitude on life was spoiled and he hated his job with a passion. The girls and I were walking on eggshells and our marriage spiraled out of control.

It was all downhill from there. I felt the ground sweep out from underneath my feet and all of the cracks split apart at the seams. Toks eventually quit his job. I was left wondering how we were going to pay the bills and continue to live in our apartment. I was doing fine with my small baking goods business and even tried to lend a hand, but he was too proud to be the man of the house accepting hand-outs from his wife.

In February 1986 everything came crashing down.

Toks shook me awake. "Wake up." He commanded.

Sleep still lingering, my eyelids fluttered as I sat up. "What's going on?"

He sat at the edge of the bed, a trail of smoke coming from the cigar between his fingers. There was a hollow look in his eyes as he stared at the wall. He looked scared. "We need to get as many things as we can carry and get out now. The landlord has not given us any more time to pay the rent and we have to leave now, right this minute". He said angrily.

I was suddenly awake, shifting upright. "Get out and go where?" My voice shook.

He *shrugged*. "I'm not sure, but we can't stay here. We need to get out of here now."

Throwing the blankets off, I shot out of bed, my heart racing in my chest. I could barely think, scarcely believe. It couldn't be true.

"What do you mean you're not sure?" I asked. "Where are we going? What's happening to our home? What about the girls?"

"The whole situation went numb and we can't stay here anymore." He got to his feet. "I'm going to my mother's house."

It was then I noticed the bag at his feet. My heart stopped, eyes wide open, going from him to the bag and back again. "Toks no. Y-you can't leave us. Please, we can still figure it all out together. We could go to counseling, please, don't leave us like this."

Silence chilled the air as he grabbed the bag and turned his back, walking away. Everything came crashing down. The Toks I saw in front of me could not be the same person I married. I never believed, in a million lifetimes, that this would happen and that the girls and I would have nowhere to go.

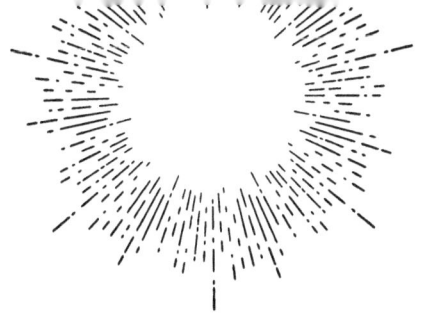

CHAPTER TWO:
A CHOICE

Have you thought about returning to Nigeria?

THAT DAY IS burned in my mind. I woke the girls from their beds, hustling around the house to stuff their suitcases with clothes, grab their backpacks and consolidate our lives into anything we could carry.

I watched two guys close the door behind us. Everything we owned, all the treasures I loved were lost behind that door. I would never see any of them again.

Standing on the street, the girls' hands in mine, I wept bitterly. How? How did I not see this coming? We stood in the middle of the street as people walked past our neighborhood smiling. I felt sorry for myself, I felt sorry for Toke and Tori, the daunting reality of being in a foreign country with no immediate means of survival weighing over me.

I was too ashamed of my circumstances to ask my family for help. Although I had two siblings who also lived in London, I was ashamed of my circumstances and cringed at the notion of being a liability to anyone. They would have so many questions with answers I wasn't ready to give. As far as everyone knew, I had the perfect family and the perfect marriage. No one knew of the problems we were having.

I had no idea what I was going to do. There were three of us. I needed time to think, to sort through the series of events unfolding at my feet. There was only one place I thought to go to, my friend Dee's house.

I knew I could count on Dee. We had been best friends forever and I felt comfortable when her name came to my mind. She was in London temporarily to give birth to her baby boy with plans to return to Nigeria soon after. She'd give it to me straight whether I wanted to hear it or not. I could cry on her shoulder and she'd be there for me without judgment, which was exactly what I needed.

This was the lowest I had felt in years and I needed my friend.

I stood in the middle of the street and watched as people walked past. I felt sorry for myself because I had nothing to smile about. I had no idea what I was going to do if for any reason Dee couldn't help me.

With my two daughters and our meager belongings in bags, we walked the distance to her apartment to unload and find rest.

"Mommy, where's daddy?" Tori asked, with tears rolling down her cheeks.

"I'm tired, can we go home?"

Tears pooled in my eyes and I tried my best to keep them from flowing. "We're almost there."

"Where are we going, mommy? Can we have our toys?" Toke asked. They were asking me questions I couldn't answer.

I squeezed their hands in mine, bristling against the onslaught of emotions threatening to overwhelm me. We got to Dee's house and knocked on her door. When she opened the door and saw us, the surprise on her face brought everything bubbling forward.

"Can you help us?" I asked, my voice cracking.

Dee smiled, glancing down at the girls, swept her door wide open, and took us inside, feeding us with grace, support, and mercy. I gave the girls a bath soon after we got to Dee's. She prepared us a hot meal and let the girls settle in her spare bedroom after the day's events caught up with them.

A heavy silence filled the air as I sat at her kitchen table. She brought a cup of chamomile tea and sat beside me, as I let the dam holding back my emotions open. For the first time, I disclosed the whole truth to someone about my relationship.

I told her everything. Toks and I were no more. The marriage had soured and there was no patching things up. The high school sweethearts were done. The saga had ended. Since that day after school, I'd had Toks to lean on and now my marriage had crumbled to the ground in a pool of ashes.

Dee was absolutely shocked. Everyone had known Toks to be successful with a good head on his shoulder. Telling her of the events of the past few months, it felt like I was talking about someone else.

A wash of relief came over me. It felt good to unload it all, the weight, the secret, the shame and get everything off my chest. I cried until the well in my eyes ran dry, clutching the cup of tea in my hands to ground myself.

"Sola," Dee said. You need to go home. You need to go home to Lagos, to Nigeria, to your origin, with your children. It would be familiar to you, you've got family there and lots of resources to get back on your feet."

I couldn't fathom it! In my mind, the prospect of returning to Nigeria was aligned with failure. I didn't want to go back there and face anyone. What would my parents, family, and friends think of me? The snide remarks, curious stares, and everyone gossiping about what happened to the "perfect couple," the inseparable sweethearts who went off to London. I thought of the people who were jealous of my relationship with Toks. I thought of how happy they would be at the news.

Even though I was caught up in an unfortunate circumstance, I was not going to accept defeat. I had not been entirely to blame for the demise of my marriage and neither had Toks. We were both to blame. I had to take responsibility for my part in the downfall. I didn't pick up on the signs in the beginning. Maybe I could have fought harder and made it work. I could have said the right things to get through to him.

That night I tossed and turned in that small bed beside my girls. Despite everything that had happened, they looked so peaceful. I was too disheveled to sleep. With eyes wide open, I prayed and asked the Lord for divine intervention. I prayed for shelter, I prayed for strength and I prayed for peace. I'd always had a deep belief in the Almighty, and now I needed him more than ever.

I didn't sleep a wink.

I got out of bed the next morning with a mix of distress and anger. Overnight I went from being bitter at my circumstances to infuriated. I could feel the smoke coming out of my ears as my mind ran in every direction. How did this happen to us? How dare our landlord take away our comfort and shelter, casting us aside like we were nothing?

Throughout my life, I always tried to be a faithful and positive person. I truly believed the more positive your thoughts, the better your life would be. Deep down, past the anger and despair, I knew I needed to turn my thoughts around for a different outcome. But the reality of our situation set in, and despite my greatest attempt, I couldn't escape the dark cloud lingering over me.

I could smell the aroma of the coffee, my mouth watering as I sat at the kitchen table. Dee finished preparing breakfast, taking a seat across from me.

"Have you thought any more about returning to Nigeria?" She asked.

My stomach twisted. I was still not convinced that returning to Nigeria was a good idea. The thought of facing everyone there still seemed terrible. "I can't go back," I answered. "The girls' school is here. Their friends are here too. We need to try and make it work here."

She took a sip of her coffee. "Well, you can try the Council."

The Council was an organization in London created to help people in my situation find shelter. My heart leaped at the mention of it, immediately sinking back down as doubt set in. We weren't residents nor were we citizens, and between Toks' engineering salary and my baking goods salary, we appeared to have it all. To the outside world, we looked upper-middle-class and The Council did not provide benefits to people who were of a presumed status.

Still, I knew I had to try. "Where can I get in touch with someone from the Council?"

Dee smiled. "I'll get the information for you."

After breakfast, I sat solemnly in meditation with my Creator. During the darkest most trying moments of my life, I would seek solace in His love. He was the only solution who could give me comfort and sound advice when I was in need.

I wept, repenting for the ugly thoughts I had towards my ex-husband, and asked for the removal of those feelings. I asked again for shelter and help during this time. A spirit of conviction followed, and he heard my cry.

I gathered the girls and our meager belongings for departure to the shelter. Dee gave me the information for the Council, embracing me and my girls as we left.

"Thank you," I said. "You've done so much for us and you're greatly appreciated."

She smiled. "I'll see you in Nigeria soon. You can meet my baby boy there."

I couldn't stomach the idea of returning home to Nigeria like this, even as we made the march from the residential areas towards bustling Central London. We journeyed by train to King's Cross, the streets buzzing with offices, shops, and restaurants.

People scurried past en route to their destinations throughout the city. Gripping my daughters' hands, I watched their wide curious eyes soak in the commotion. King's Cross was known as a transportation hub, trains zipping in and out in all directions across the country.

On the outskirts of the established areas were the seedier areas of King's Cross, where the Council was located. I held the girls close to me as we made our way to the building, muttering prayers as I rang the doorbell.

I could hear the rushed, thundering footsteps behind the door before the man answered. He was middle-aged, with sloppy, dirty blond hair obscuring his eyes. He smiled awkwardly at us. A half-eaten sandwich in his hand and mustard in his unkempt beard, he cleared his throat and swallowed.

"I'm sorry," he said. "I wasn't expecting anyone." His eyes drifted to the two small hands I was holding and he stepped to the side. "Please, come in."

I tried to smile politely back at him as we entered. We followed him down a narrow, damp hallway, the walls lined with brick and numbered doors. Faint light bulbs dangled from the ceiling barely lighting the space in front of us to see. I could hear the pitter-patter of shoes throughout the floor as we entered his office.

Plopping down into his brown leather chair, he squeezed his beer belly up against the desk and set his sandwich down on the paper.

"Um, you have some mustard..." I trailed off and motioned to his chin.

He laughed nervously, wiping his face with a napkin as I stood in front of his desk, my daughters peering out from behind my legs.

"How can I help you?" he asked.

I explained the entire situation to him, and he proceeded to ask me a series of questions, taking notes on his pad. Where did you live before coming here? Why are you homeless? Are you married, divorced, or separated? How old are your children? Do you have any sources of income? I engaged him with answers as best as I could, watching the expression on his face shift.

He cleared his throat. "I'm sorry ma'am, I'm not sure if my organization is going to be able to help you." I choked back the tears that threatened to spill over. I knew this was my only chance. I had to get through to him, I had to get him to help us.

I met his eyes. "If you place us back on the streets, then that is where we will be."

I saw a look of compassion flash through his eyes and his expression softened, looking down at my girls and back up at me.

"You don't have to sleep on the streets, ma'am. I will help you." He walked toward me and smiled warmly. "How could I say no to these precious, little faces? Give me a moment to see what we have available."

I would've never dreamt my life would come to this moment. I was homeless, standing in a rundown building begging for a nice man to help me. It didn't feel real. My anger swelled inside me. My husband was tucked away comfortably at his mother's house with regular hot meals and a warm bed, while the girls and I were pleading for shelter from the cold.

He took us to a gloomy, disheveled building with fans in the windows, clothes strung across the balconies to dry, and the sounds of televisions screaming from every window. I could smell bacon and eggs in the hallway as he gave us the key to the bedroom and left us to settle in.

It was a dark and dingy two-bedroom apartment with a mother and her son in the other bedroom. I learned she was a victim of domestic violence and had fled her home to escape her husband. She kept to herself and stayed locked in her room most of the time.

The tiny apartment felt hollow like it had been vacant for a while before we came. It was furnished with the bare basics, a few pots and pans, a towel, a couch, and a dining room table. The walls were all painted the same dull tan, with no decorations or color anywhere in sight.

I thought of my beautiful African pieces, the art and antiques left at my old home, and where I would've put them if I had brought them with me. The girls huddled together, holding hands as they followed me back towards the bedroom.

There was one double bed in the center of the room. No chairs, drawers, or closets to put our things in. A cramped bathroom was tucked to one side with a meek sink and a single roll of toilet paper. There wasn't a refrigerator to store food or any places for cups or cutlery, so I used the windowsill to store them. I needed to change the lightbulb in the room, and would have to buy a space heater if we wanted any additional warmth.

For breakfast, we had bread with butter and marmalade, or cereal with powdered milk. Eventually, I got the girls enrolled back in school and they were able to have lunch there. Most days, I skipped lunch to put the money towards dinner. We had Chinese Rice with vegetables every night. That was quite available.

This uncomfortable situation was all I had to provide for me and the girls, and I was thankful to have somewhere to lay our heads. We weren't homeless anymore and we still had each other. I hoped the girls would adjust to their new school and make new friends, I knew we wouldn't stay here for long. I wouldn't allow it. It was a far cry from where we'd come from but together we'd get through this.

Life at the shelter was hectic and stressful during the day, and frightening at night. The room next to ours was the bar for the shelters and a lot of eccentric characters came and went throughout the night. From Monday through Saturday it stayed open from 6 p.m. to 4 a.m., although more often than not, it didn't close until 5 a.m.

Loud music beat through the walls and profanity was shouted to compete with the noise. At all hours of the night, drunk men would lose their way and start banging on our doors, lurching us from sleep at the disturbance. The girls being young and still not fully aware of our situation would always fall back asleep, where most nights were sleepless for me. A lot of times, drunks would pass out at our doorstep and I'd leave our door closed until they woke several hours later and continued on their way.

This made it difficult for us to get up at 6 a.m., rested and ready for the day ahead. Every day, the girls took four buses each way to and from school. We were up early trekking between stops before a full day of school activities even started. After a long journey home in the evening, they did their homework, had dinner, took their bath, and sank into bed, exhausted.

Most mornings, I pushed Tori in her stroller down the sidewalk towards the bus stop, tightly holding Toke's hand, pulling her close to me against the cold chill that swept down the street.

One very cold morning, Toke burst into tears. She let go of my hand and sank onto the ice-cold concrete. "Please mommy please don't make me go to school anymore. I don't like it there. I don't like the kids there because they don't play with me. I miss my friends at the other school.

I miss all my dolls and toys. I miss my room. I miss our old house. I miss my daddy too. I want to go back home mommy please, I'm begging you," she cried.

It wasn't until that moment that I felt the full weight of everything sink over me. I looked at my weary daughter and felt the exhaustion I'd been ignoring finally come up. She was tired, and so was I.

I scooped her into my arms, fighting back my own tears. "Don't worry, I'm going to change your school, I promise. I'll move us out of that place very soon. Everything is going to be fine, I promise."

She gave me a half-hearted smile and tight hug before we continued on the rest of our journey. It wasn't until they were safely inside the school that I finally allowed myself to cry. I wept the entire journey back to the shelter, letting everything flow over and out of me that I'd been holding inside.

I knew I had to leave London and go back to Nigeria. We couldn't stay at that homeless shelter anymore. Dee was right, I needed family, resources, and the warmth of home. I was finally ready to face Nigeria.

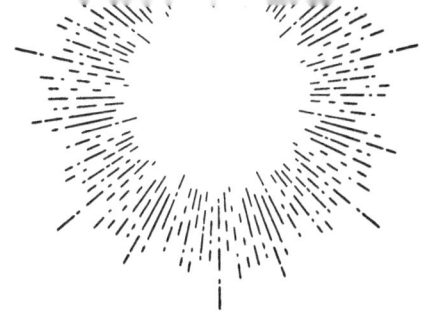

CHAPTER THREE:
THE VOYAGE

Nigerian tribes differ in religion, faith, practices, and lifestyles. Art from different cultures exhibits unique characteristics. Every tribe has its own cuisine, fashion style, and festival.

SINCE I WAS a little girl I had dreams about visiting other countries, especially Europe and the United States of America. After Toks and I started dating, we would spend hours on the phone, talking about the day we would leave and explore the world together. We wanted to raise our children somewhere like London or the United States. The day Toks and I left was filled with celebration and infinite possibilities. I was leaving to make something positive of myself and see the world with the love of my life.

It was hard to believe the girls and I were now going back to Lagos, without my husband, their dad.

I knew it was time for me to return home to Nigeria. Staying in London was no longer feasible for me. Seeing my daughters weary and unhappy coupled with my depleting resources meant I could no longer ignore the reality. I'd fought Dee at every turn when she advised me to return home, but deep down I knew she was right.

I had wrestled with returning to Nigeria for weeks, fighting my own internal sense of failure. I couldn't help but feel like I had failed in every way, in my marriage, and in my community. In London, I had been very involved in community efforts as head of our women's book club and parent-school programs. I had worked tirelessly to build my business and provide a warm and vibrant space for my family to grow and thrive. All that had been ripped out from underneath me.

Deep in my heart of hearts, I knew I wasn't a failure. I had been forced to live in the shelter with my two beautiful children without their father, the man that we loved and loved us. Every day I communed with my Creator for guidance, support and direction, and

He never failed me. I had to believe everything would turn out for the best, it was the only hope I had amidst the daily struggle to keep the faith. I knew my girls were watching me, watching my reactions, searching for strength and direction from me. I wanted them to see me as a strong woman. I would not let them see me break down. I could not let them down. During our last few weeks in London, I scaled everything back to living only on the bare necessities. We had a long way home to Africa. It was my first time traveling by myself with the girls. I didn't want us to be bogged down with a lot of items to make the trip more difficult.

My cousin who lived in London gave me the money I needed to purchase the three one-way tickets to Lagos. I'll forever be grateful to her for aiding us in our time of need. It was time to go home to our family and vacate our room at the shelter for another soul in need.

The young woman and her little boy that we shared the shelter apartment with had moved out earlier, returning to Florida to be with her family. As I gathered our three small suitcases, our entire lives compressed into what we could carry, I glanced around the dark empty apartment. It was a far cry from the sprawling Hampstead apartment we'd shared with Toks which seemed like ages ago. We hadn't heard from him since he walked away that last day. He never looked back, and now neither would I.

The girls and I said goodbye to our small bedroom in the shelter and made our way to the airport. As we waited on the steps of the shelter for our taxi, I watched the sun come up over King's Cross with a cup of steaming coffee in my hand. The rain that carried overnight had subsided and a beautiful day was breaking over the city. I couldn't help but wonder, did I ever know the real Toks? All of those years together, when did they stop meaning something? If they ever meant anything at all.

Would I ever find love again? Would I know what it looked like if it walked up to me someday, somewhere? Everything I thought I knew had disappeared in a moment. I'd thought what Toks and I had was love, but in the end, I didn't even recognize the man I married.

Just as my mind began to wander, the taxi breaks squeaked to a stop in front of the doorstep. We scrambled into action, rousing the drowsy girls and hurrying them to grab their suitcases.

"Good morning!" The older man called as he jogged towards us, his voice thick with an accent. He grabbed the suitcases from my daughters, a jovial smile on his face.

With salt and pepper hair, and wrinkles along the caramel skin on his face, he closed the door behind me and made his way to the front seat. The warm air smelled of coffee and peppermint as we departed the shelter en route to our future.

As we made our way along the highways towards the airport, he filled the cab with stories of his family. His loving wife and their beautiful daughter who was in medical school. With a smile, he glanced at the pictures on his dashboard, telling me of his grandchildren and their wonderful family.

The girls easily fell asleep.They were so exhausted. I listened casually, and for the first time in what felt like ages, a smile lifted along my cheeks. He didn't pepper me with questions, and I realized how grateful I was not to have to explain myself. Listening to him, I felt my mind sigh in relief, I wasn't thinking about what to say, how to say it, I could simply be and listen.

Throughout the frequent stops in traffic and waiting bumper to bumper with dozens of other early morning travelers, he continued with gentle stories, a perpetual smile on his face. Somewhere in the middle of it all, I fell asleep too.

As we pulled into the airport drop-off, he woke me up and I gently roused the girls. Couples were kissing their loved ones goodbye as we reached the curb and grabbed our suitcases from the trunk. As I thanked the driver for a lovely trip, he gave me his business card with a smile.

"Anytime you need a taxi, call me. I will come and get you." Waving goodbye to the girls and me, he got back inside the cab to continue on his way.

We had a long flight to Lagos, where my dear brother would be waiting to pick us up. Soon we'd be back at home surrounded by people who loved us. I intentionally let the subtle relief set in before entering the airport.

Keeping the girls close, my mind couldn't help but drift to the thought of Toks asleep at his mother's house in a comfortable bed, as if we, his family, had never existed. Before, when we had traveled together, Toks and I had a motto, "Team work makes the dream work." We would each take one of the girls' hands and make our way through security and boarding. We lovingly did everything together, as a happy family.

After standing in line for what felt like hours, I hurried to grab the girls' bags for security to check. Managing them both was much harder alone, but I did my best to keep everything moving. We had arrived early to check in our bags, which freed up my hands and allowed us some time before settling down for the long flight home.

I took each of the girls by the hand and led them through the airport, their eyes bulging wide as they whipped their heads to all sides to take in everything. The hustling passengers, flight attendants, massive ceilings, and murals lining the walls.

I guided them to a small restaurant for breakfast. I'd managed to save a reserve of money for when we made it to Nigeria. I still wasn't prepared to ask for shelter or money and wanted to provide as much as we could for ourselves.

Different photos of iconic locations hung from the restaurant walls, like the Buckingham Palace, the Tower of London, Big Ben, the London Eye, etc. I didn't know if

I would ever return to London, or what the future might hold, but I would never forget this chapter of my life. I could not believe I was leaving everything behind - the beautiful life we had in London, the love I thought I had known and everything I wanted.

As the girls shared their plate of food, I pulled an empty notebook from my bag. During the journey, I planned to use the time to write down all of my thoughts on how I was going to settle us down once I got to Nigeria.

I knew Toks' sister was still in Lagos and had two girls around the same age as mine. They had only seen each other in pictures, and despite everything going on, they were family. Would she even accept my visitation request? There was no telling what Toks told her or anyone in his family about me and our impending divorce. Nothing I could hear about him would surprise me anymore. I wrote her name in my notebook.

After breakfast, we began the long walk from one end of the airport to our gate all the way on the other side. I alternated carrying each of my daughters a short distance after they grew tired of walking.We stopped periodically to rest before finally arriving at the waiting area.

A cacophony of voices filled the space as people milled out about the open area talking amongst themselves, reading the newspaper, or working on their computers. I found two seats closer to the runway agent, Toke sat on one seat while I sat on the other seat with Tori on my lap.

We would each have our own seats on the flight. My bag was full of coloring books, books, crayons, and other things to keep the girls engaged for most of the journey. I hoped they would fall asleep at some point and wake up with the past behind them.

The flight attendant called for boarding and we made our way into the stream of people funneling past the gate and into the airplane. After the girls were comfortably seated in their seats, with their safety belts fastened, I settled in for the journey home.

I still remember the butterflies in my stomach as I sat next to Toks en route to our new life in London. The questions ran through my head, the anticipation, and my thoughts drifted to Nigeria. Would it look the same as before? How much would have changed after all these years? How would we be welcomed by our family and friends? I was sure word had already traveled around town that Toks and I would be getting a divorce, and that I was coming back to Lagos with the girls.

How was I going to explain why Toks and I weren't together anymore? What was I supposed to say when someone asked where he was? I wasn't ready to answer questions and still wanted to keep a level of privacy in my marriage if that was possible.

I knew my childhood friends would not shun me and things would quickly go back to the way they used to be. Even though we slowly drifted away from each other as we continued on with our lives, we kept in touch and checked on each other from time to time. I had called Temi after things fell apart with Toks and I. Just like when we were younger, she listened to all I had to say and never told me that she had warned me. She lived in the United States with her husband Tunde and their three beautiful children. I couldn't help but wonder how different my life would have been if I'd listened to her on the way home from school all those years ago.

Peering out the window as our flight was descending, I saw the glittering lights of Lagos illuminating the dark coast. Nigeria is called "The Heartbeat of Africa." Vast in wondrous landscapes of rolling hills, sweeping rivers, waters from the gulf filling the lagoons, mountains, and lush greenery. A beautiful, multicultural West African hub, Nigeria's culture perfectly juxtaposes the antiquity of traditional methods and structures like the oldest dye pit in Africa, with the rapid growth of the modern industry as the world's second largest film production center, Nollywood.

The girls and I were headed back to my home, the largest city and former capital of Nigeria, Lagos. I felt my excitement brewing. My daughters would be able to experience the beauty and wonder of their homeland, like the Lagos Street Carnival and One Lagos Fiesta. People filled the streets, brilliant colors flashing as we danced for days to the music of the different tribes in Lagos. The Yoruba of the southwest, the Igbo of the southeast, the Edo of the Midwest and the Hausa and Fulani tribes to the north.

Every tribe had its own culture, cuisine, fashion, and festivals that all came under the sprawling umbrella of Lagos. There would be no shortage of things for the girls to explore and experience once we arrived home. I wanted them to see all of Nigeria's beauty and splendor. The Olumo rock in Abeokuta my hometown, the Zuma rock, the Erin Ijesha Waterfall, the Kofar Mata Dye Pit in Kano, established in 1498, the traditional methods of carving art works in northern Nigeria, etc. The methods and skills employed are ancient and have been passed down through generations.

In a country of about 200 million people, 250 ethnicities, 500 languages, and 36 states, we lived at the heart of it all.

The flight went smoothly with the girls sleeping for most of the trip. I spent my time writing in my notebook. My head was about to explode from all of the thoughts I had been keeping locked inside. I had seven hours to pour them out, write them all down and sort through them all. By the end of it, I was optimistic and had a renewed sense of purpose. As we filed off the plane and retrieved our bags from the carousel, my heart skipped a beat. My brother was going to be there waiting for us, to take us home to our family. Growing up he had always been my protector before my relationship with Toks. He always looked out for me, and I knew he was not going to be happy when I told him the details of my failed marriage.

I saw my brother leaning against his car through the glass doors and fought the urge to run to him. He looked taller and thinner with huge muscles bulging out of his shirt. As we stepped outside, I gave in, clutching the girls' hands as we ran into his arms and hugged for what seemed like a lifetime.

I took a deep breath, allowing that moment to last. The relief and familiarity of being held by my dear brother, my best friend, who always protected me since I was a little girl made me feel better. I was home. I felt safe for the first time since Toks and I parted ways. It was a beautiful feeling.

He swept the girls off their feet, a chorus of giggles and exclamations filling the loading zone at the airport. We had arrived late at night, and despite the weariness from the long flight, I was more overjoyed than I had been in a long time.

We got into the car and he whisked us away from the airport towards home. My parents still lived in the home where we all grew up. Toke, Tori and I would stay in my old bedroom. My brother, his wife, and their three kids lived in the same compound, in the three bedroom bungalow my father had built behind the main house. My two brothers had lived there before they left home for college.

My family was close-knit and no matter what was going on at any time with any of us, we stuck by each other. My father was a great family man. He was loving and God fearing. He worked hard and made sure we lacked nothing. He was very generous and was always ready to help any extended family members who needed help. My mother was and still is a very strong loving woman who gives great advice. You can talk to her about anything and she'll listen to you without fear of being judged, no matter how bad your story is. In her late 90s, I still call her every day to check on her and ask her for solutions to problems. She's very loving, prayerful and full of wisdom.

I never wanted to tell my parents Toks and I were getting a divorce. They loved him like a son and were so pleased when we first started dating. They thought we were the perfect match, and so did I. Everyone did.

Without hesitation, they offered for us to stay with them until I got my own place and a job. My mom was able to enroll the girls into a private school two weeks after we arrived in Lagos. The school was five miles away from home. They were dropped off and picked up by my father's driver and my mother's house keeper every day. They had to start school right away so their education wasn't thwarted because of any setbacks. It was not easy settling down at their new school but they adjusted and loved it.

With the relief I felt when I settled down at my parents' home, I finally understood what Dee had been telling me from the start. In Nigeria, I was home, and when I was home I was never alone.

The girls were so happy to be at their grandparents' house. They were amazing. They were loving, attentive, and showered their granddaughters with hugs and kisses. My Mom woke up early every morning, cooking and humming, making me feel like coming back home was the best thing to do. As we awoke to each new day, the house would be filled with breakfast aromas and fresh coffee. I would offer my assistance but she would tell me to get out of the kitchen and let her cook. At ninety-six years old, this beautiful mother of mine is still the best cook I know.

My parents were both disciplinarians. My father, a Preacher and a Church leader at our local church made sure we went to church every Sunday. He loved his wife very much and doted on his children. He was an only child and decided on having a big family which brought him so much joy.

As we drove through the bright streets of Lagos at night, I watched the buildings pass by, the girls fast asleep in the backseat. Out of the window, I saw the NECOM building, new development and existing neighborhoods. In my bag, I clutched my notebook and felt that swell of optimism surge inside me.

I was going to restart my baking goods business. I knew how to make necklaces and bracelets. I could catapult that into my baking goods business. There was a huge bead store near the bar beach on Lagos island. There I could purchase materials to make my beautifully designed necklaces and bracelets. I could sell them to my friends, family members, and fashion stores. The possibilities were endless and for the first time since this all began, things didn't seem so dire. There was hope. My girls and I would be just fine.

I could feel Nigeria welcoming me back home. Back to my essence. Back to where I belonged.

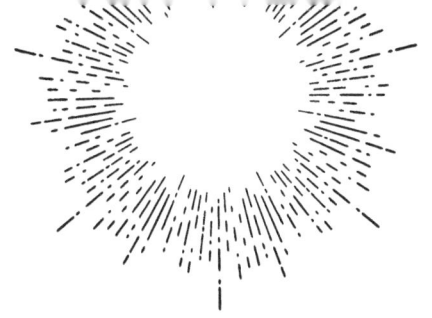

CHAPTER FOUR:
ROBBERIES IN NIGERIA

I was shocked when I became a victim
of the robberies in broad daylight.

AS WE DROVE through the streets of Lagos, I felt the familiar comfort of home, seeing the streets of the city where I grew up.

"Hey," my brother said, his voice low not to wake the girls in the backseat. "I want you to be very careful going into town. Things aren't like they used to be before you left."

I frowned. "What do you mean?"

"People have been getting brutally beaten in the streets and robbed of their possessions. Sometimes they go missing. Every night on the news, there are new victims."

I was stunned and speechless. The Nigeria I'd returned to had changed terribly in so many ways.

Over the years, crime motivated by economical and political reasons has risen. Gangs and criminal groups have always existed, but they have grown and become more sophisticated and dangerous as crime has become a lucrative industry.

Kidnapping thrives because it pays. Bandits and criminals have extorted millions of dollars from poor and struggling families throughout the country. Oftentimes they are more organized, armed, and equipped than many law enforcement agencies with a heavy military operation behind these crimes. There are dense, mountainous forests that have been mismanaged for years, creating the perfect hideout for bandits to take their abducted victims unnoticed and hold them there.

The Nigerian government has had a difficult time apprehending these criminals and citizens are afraid to speak out and leave their homes for fear of being targeted. Investigations are at a dead end, leaving these people to continue their criminal behavior. Police reports are filed only to never appear before a court or have any charges presented; criminals receive no punishment for their crimes and there has been little justice.

Due to the profitable nature of these crimes, corruption, and bribery in the country are on the rise. Security forces are overworked, underpaid, and under-equipped, making it easy for kidnappings to continue to occur. Robbers strike anywhere at any time. There is no security, no recourse. These bad guys kill for fun.

There have been community meetings and programs set up by various Nigerian organizations and activists to combat these crimes. Television coverage, marches, and community events are crying for help. These crimes have forced many Nigerians to flee the country to other countries near and far!

It is as though these bandits have taken over my country and there is no one to stop them.

Due to the robberies, I did not venture out onto the streets as I used to when I was younger. I stayed home as much as I could. If there was no reason to go outdoors, I did not. Staying at home did not stop one from being robbed. I was robbed at my apartment three different times in seven months. Each time I was robbed, I would tighten up security. Nowhere was safe. Most of the robberies were in-house, mostly planned by the maids and drivers. I opted for a pay-as-you-go driver and housekeeper. My worst experience of being robbed was when I became a victim of a robbery in broad daylight, at two o'clock in the afternoon!!!

The sun shimmered over Lagos as I opened the curtains to our apartment. We'd been home in Nigeria for a little while and decided to leave my parents' house for a rented apartment not too far away from them. I had also gotten myself a little compact car and a driver who reported for work whenever I needed him. I didn't go out too often. I worked from home, baking and decorating cakes.

Every morning the girls and I would have our quiet time together, shower, get dressed, eat a quick breakfast, before dropping them off at school. One beautiful Thursday morning, I had some errands to run on the Island, my favorite place to unwind and also do all my grocery shopping. In the heat of summer, I wanted to be comfortable while I was out, opting for a strapless, yellow floral dress and a matching pair of flat sandals.

Purse in hand, I headed out the door. Our neighbors smiled at me as I passed, giving them a friendly wave as I made my way to my car. Sunlight gleaming in my eyes, I happily sang along to the music coming from my radio, driving towards the third mainland bridge to Lagos Island.

My cell phone buzzed in my purse and I turned down the radio station to answer.

"Hey Sola," my sister's voice rang through the other end of the phone. "You're still coming with me to that party this weekend, right? There are going to be some nice guys there. It's going to be fun with nice people, good music, and plenty to eat and drink."

I rolled my eyes and smiled. "I'll be there, but I'm not ready to meet anyone yet. So please forget about introducing anyone to me. I will not show up if that's your plan." I told her.

We chatted for a few minutes, exchanged pleasantries and said our goodbyes as I pulled into the parking lot of Hancock Shopping Mall in Lekki. Hancock Mall is a nice place for purchasing everything you need - including groceries.

My sister Ayo had been on my case about finding someone and moving on from Toks, but I'd been hesitant to put myself back out there. He hadn't crossed my mind as much lately. The girls and I were happy and doing just fine on our own. I wanted to protect what we had.

The Mall buzzed as people scurried between the shops to get to their destinations. Little children ran around their parents' legs, a chorus of giggles as their parents tried to keep them orderly. Elderly folks walked slowly going from one shop to another, checking out dresses and shoes but not buying anything. They were just out to get some fresh air, bond with each other and have a great time. I love watching the oldies, especially when they're holding hands, going for a walk, talking softly and lovingly looking at each other's faces. My parents were always my favorite couple to watch until my father passed on several years ago.

On the other side of the Mall, a carnival had come into town for the upcoming holiday festivities. A huge Ferris wheel spun above the various rides, with games, and food stands scattered everywhere. A smile swept across my face.

The girls would love this fun place. I could picture them hollering and screaming in delight, with the tilt-a-whirl spinning them around and around.

I pushed into the crowded grocery store, hurrying through the aisle to find my items. People were picking over the fruits and vegetables getting everything they needed for the upcoming festivities. I wanted to find the best ones out of the bunch.

Standing in the long lines, I chatted with other patrons while waiting. I paid for my items before heading to the shoe store. Toke, Toni and I needed some new shoes. I grabbed them two pairs of pink Mickey Mouse sneakers before taking my time to find myself a pair of shoes.

After finding a pair of traditional, black low heels, I decided to take my time to walk around the Mall with my new shoes on. Maybe I could wear them to the party Ayo had invited me to. A gentle breeze swept through the crowded walkways, carrying the scents of the food stalls and the buzz of conversation throughout the open Mall.

I stopped for some popcorn and a bottle of water before finding a warm shaded spot on a bench outside to sit, enjoy my snack and relax. I watched the people pass by, the different dialects and tribes all intermingled. The upcoming festival would fill the streets with music, dancing, and food from all over the country. In our short time here, the girls had already gotten to experience so much of home. They were getting settled in their school and had already made friends in our community. It was such a nice day, I was not ready to leave but it was almost time to pick the girls up from school.

After observing the people passing by and my popcorn now gone, I decided to head back to the Mainland. Shopping bags in hand, I headed towards my car, my mind swept up in thinking of what I would cook for dinner.

I didn't see them until they were all around me and it was too late.

"Give us the bags!" one of them shouted, pointing the gun barrel at me.

I couldn't see his face behind the mask, only hard brown eyes without so much a glimmer of remorse. Before I could open my mouth to tell him no, I felt the blunt metal slam against the back of my head, my vision going white and I tumbled to the ground, muddy water splashing all over me.

Four robbers were all over me, scrambling for my purse and shopping bags. I screamed, hoping someone would hear me. People heard! People watched! No one came close for fear of being shot. One of them punched me in the face.

"Shut up!" he shouted.

They took everything - my wristwatch, my jewelry, and my purse with the car and house keys inside. I was too stunned to move, my head throbbing. I heard the car doors close and they sped off. I didn't fully understand what was happening at the time, too stunned by the severity of events and the pain in my skull.

When I was fully conscious of what just happened, it was complete chaos.

"Call the police!" someone shouted. I was hoping to hear, "call the ambulance."

Another person grabbed my arm and pulled me out of the puddle, my dress soaked with muddy brown water.

"Are you ok?" someone else asked. What a stupid question I thought.

I felt the knot in my head throb, burning heat rushing through my eye and down my cheeks. I was confused, terrified. I needed to get to a hospital.

"They...they took my car. All of my things," I managed to say, looking at the older woman's kind face staring back at me.

"I saw the whole thing!" someone else exclaimed.

One of the good samaritans helped me into his car and drove me to a nearby hospital. The entire time he consoled me, his voice quiet and calm as he spoke.

"When you get out of the hospital, let the police know what happened to you. If you're lucky, they may help you." He was an older man with slicked-back hair and a long beard, his freshly manicured nails gripping the steering wheels. "I can't believe we've had another robbery here so soon. Someone needs to do something about these people."

He was going on and on about how the police were not doing anything and how we were living in a country with this nonsense. As he swore under his breath, I knew I needed to get to a phone as soon as possible. I had to call my family to tell them what happened to me. The girls also had to be picked up from school. The Good Samaritan gave me his phone. I called and managed to speak to my mom who was anxious to get to where I was. I refused to tell her. All I wanted her to do was to pick the girls up from school. By the time we got to the hospital, I was soaked in blood!

The commotion of the hospital aggravated the throbbing in my head. I heard car horns as they pulled in and out, hospital staff frantically coming and going. I sank into one of the waiting room chairs as this kind man went to the reception to check me in. He was waving his hands back and forth in disgust at my unfortunate situation as he described what happened. After doing all he could to help me, he walked over to where I was seated and I thanked him. He patted me on my back, told me he was running late for a very important meeting and left. I was so grateful to this kind-hearted stranger and a few minutes later, I realized I never asked for his name.

I surveyed the hospital waiting room. Across from me, a mother cradled her son's arm, I assumed he'd broken it. Cries, coughs, chatter, and sniffles filled the area. People in pain were hanging around, waiting to be seen while the nurse at the reception was loudly popping her gum from time to time. The waiting room door swung open and closed as physicians walked out to their next patients. One physician smiled at me as she walked past with a cup of coffee in her hand, not saying a word to me. I expected her to show some compassion, get someone to help me, seeing I was covered in blood!

After waiting a long time, I was called in to be cleaned up and later led to the X-ray room to check if I had any fractures. It was a long process going from test to test and answering a lot of questions. I got the basic treatment I needed and was given a prescription for pain medication. I asked a young man if there was a police station nearby where I could go and file a report. He shrugged his shoulders and walked away from me, without saying a word. One of the nurses later told me it would be better to go to the police station closest to my house where it would be easier for me to get to, each time I was summoned to report there. I knew my cries for justice would probably go unanswered because very few of the victims had received justice for these types of crimes. Many victims joined forces with local news reporters to demand justice, often appearing on television. The criminals were masked, and those that could identify them were not talking. I hoped I would be wrong in my assumption about law enforcement regarding my case.

The robbers had my purse with my house keys, money, and all of my identification in it. They knew where I lived. Unnerved, I wanted it all to just go away and instantly knew I was going to be moving out of Lagos. Enough was enough. I couldn't take all these robberies anymore. There would be no justice and I had to find a way to move on with my life. I had family and friends in the United States who could help me get on my feet. I could enroll the girls in a better school, make new friends and start a new adventure. London was also a possibility, I knew the city and could start over there. I later decided against moving to London because there were too many negative memories and I was not willing to re-open past wounds. The more I thought about it, the better the United States sounded. It was beautiful there and the girls would absolutely love it.

I knew my parents would not be pleased with me moving again based on everything the girls and I had been through before we moved back home. However, I could not live in a city where I had been robbed several times and almost got killed during the last robbery. I lived in fear inside and outside my home. I had sleepless nights and was always tired. I had to do what was best for myself and my daughters. The girls were safely home when I got home. Thank goodness I had given a copy of the apartment key to my mother when we moved in. My father had released his driver to take my mother to pick the girls up. She had given them their snack and was helping with their homework. I was very grateful and thanked her. She was sorry and very angry at what had happened to me. "When will all this nonsense stop?" my mom asked. The girls ran towards me, broke down in tears, and were all over me. They bombarded me with questions but I was not in the mood to talk. I was scared, still very angry, and in so much pain. Nicely, I pleaded with them that I needed to rest. It had been a long day, with a horrible experience. I was exhausted. I just wanted to be left alone.

I went to my room, closed the door, and immediately called my friend Tomi who lived in Atlanta, Georgia. I wanted to check with her and get her thoughts on my moving there. As the phone rang, I thought about how we met and became such good friends. We had met her and Brian her husband, in London, at "Our Souls Church" where we worshipped every Sunday. Brian had gotten a great job with an American company in Atlanta. We missed them so much but still called each other occasionally. I was glad I was still able to contact her, especially at this time!

She picked up quickly.

"Hello, this is Tomi."

"Hi Tomi, this is Sola!" From the tone of my voice, she knew immediately that something was wrong and asked. I went straight to the point and told her that "I am thinking of moving to the United States with my daughters."

I could hear the excitement in Tomi's voice, "Yes! I am so happy to hear that! That's great news. We've missed you guys. The girls will love it here and so will you. Life is so good here. When are you thinking of coming?"

I paused for a moment to think about that question, "I am thinking of coming within the next three months and I wanted to know if the girls and I could stay with you guys until we get ourselves situated?"

In the voice I knew so well she replied, "Yes, of course".

"And Brian? Will Brian be fine with us staying with you for a while?" I muttered.

"He loves your family so much like you're his blood. He has a good spirit, the reason I said YES when he proposed to me those years ago". I knew Brian to be a very kind human being, always there to help whoever needed it. But I still needed to know it would be fine with him. He deserved that respect from me. I was happy and grateful to the Lord for this friendship. The plan was set and I decided to take the leap of faith and move to Atlanta. I did not want to take any more chances of being a victim with no justice served. It was crazy. It was sinful!

In keeping up with Tomi I learned there was a huge market for baking and selling African dresses and I could really make a good living. Six weeks after Tomi and I spoke, the girls and I left Lagos. We left in tears because of the loving family and friends we were leaving behind. But I was happy to be moving out of this danger zone, the place I had loved and called home, where I almost got killed! The flight to Atlanta was long, a good twelve-hour flight! All I thought about was what lay ahead. Another move, a new beginning. Placing our future in the Lord's hands, I knew all would be well with me, Toke and Tori.

We were met at the airport by my Tomi. We laughed and cried for joy. The ride to the house was smooth, unlike the ones I got used to in Lagos. We got to our new temporary home where we were welcomed with warmth and love by Brian. It was a beautiful three-bedroom home in Decatur Georgia, about twenty miles from Atlanta. I was pleased Tomi took me around to meet her many friends in her neighborhood and in Atlanta. I also called my old friends and made sure I visited them to get reacquainted. I developed a great inner circle of people I could be friendly with and maybe trust. I knew I wouldn't mind living in the neighborhood so I felt comfortable with Tomi helping to enroll the girls at the middle school not too far away from her house.

We were at Tomi's house for two months before we moved into a lovely two-bedroom apartment ten minutes away. The girls were picked up and dropped off by the school bus every day, a luxury we did not have in Lagos. It was so convenient and I loved the fact that I would be free for a few hours before school was over. My car became my mobile shop. I regularly drove for hours to show people my beautiful collection of dresses I had brought from Nigeria to sell. I got orders of cakes and pies which were baked in the evenings after the girls went to bed.

One fine morning, I was feeling happy and decided to walk around the neighborhood. It was Spring. The trees were budding and the air was crisp. Winter was weaning away and signs of upcoming warmth and sunny days were everywhere. It was a gorgeous green neighborhood with houses lined into subdivisions. The trees were huge outlining the streets and there was no shortage of restaurants or stores to satisfy every need and want. This beautiful morning, as I was walking through the neighborhood, I opted to take a left turn instead of my normal right turn and saw a massive, beautiful building. It was so beautiful I had to catch my breath. It resembled a cathedral with its gold and red trimmings and high towers. It stood tall among the trees and called me over. I went to the grounds to take a better look and was filled with joy while standing there. A peaceful energy washed over me and I knew I had to come back. I had to see inside this beauty. The energy I felt was like an ocean washing over the rocks. It felt good. I wanted to meet who was behind these beautiful gold doors. This church filled me with peace and joy. I looked at the sign on the door to see the times for the services. Sunday service was at eleven o'clock in the morning. I promised myself to go back there to worship.

On the following Sunday, I woke up early and prepared for worship. The girls were all dressed in their pink dresses, bows, and pigtails. I made sure they understood the importance of behaving in church before we stepped foot on the grounds. The smiling faces when we arrived were overwhelming but pleasant. Walking through the front door, a young man was there to open the door for us. He had a fresh haircut, big brown eyes, and wore a black suit. You could tell he was proud to be there, opening the door for congregants this Sunday.

While he smiled at me, an elderly lady walked up and greeted us with a beautiful smile and warmly said, "Welcome! It is guaranteed to be a great service as always!"

She wore a white skirt suit and a white big hat. I could see curls peering down out of the sides of the hat. I stopped and took in the beautiful sight, people were hurrying in to find their seats and some were off to the side conversing with one another. Kids ran up and down the front corridor as their parents yelled for them to behave. On the right side was a bookstore filled with religious books and gift items. At the back of the bookstore was a coffee shop named "Spirituality." On the left side were the stairs to the balcony, offices, and restrooms. The doors into the sanctuary were directly in front of us. As I took note of where the restrooms were located, I was asked if it was my first time there by a middle-aged man. I told him, "yes" and happily, he handed me a program and I was escorted to my seat with the girls holding my hands. A beautiful young lady in a red dress explained to me that the girls had to go with her to the children's service in the basement. The girls hugged me and left with smiles on their young innocent faces.

I took a good look at the church which was breathtaking. There were huge gold pillars lining the church from front to back. The windows were blue and red. The church floors were adorned with red and gold rugs and the seats were a red couch style. It was a huge church. On the back of the seat in front of me was a bookcase with a Bible and hymn book. Everything about the church was welcoming and I decided to join this church family and become a member. Two weeks after I became a member, I signed up to become a worker ushering people in and collecting offerings. After a couple of weeks, I took some of my baked goodies to the coffee shop for a tasting. The lady at the coffee shop was really nice and asked me to bring cupcakes and pies to the coffee shop every Sunday. I had earlier explained to her that I needed the extra cash. Each Sunday, after church, I gave cupcakes and pies to some people who could not afford to spend the extra dollar and sold them to people who could afford to pay. A percentage always went back to the church. Wearing my lovely African dresses to church got me a huge clientele of people interested in buying my authentic African clothes. I was led by the spirit to this beautiful church "Cathedral of the Holy Spirit" pastored by a white family with predominantly black worshipers. We were one big happy family. I loved this church and so did the girls.

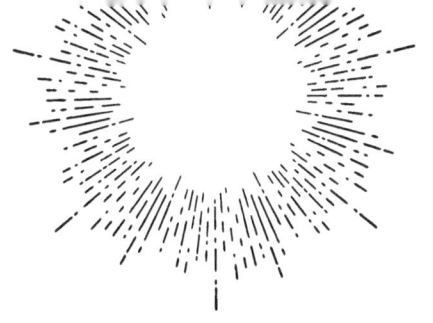

CHAPTER FIVE:
FARIDA'S STORY

It was as if the sun was my constant companion, following me, guiding my car up the highway to the address I had been given. It was a beautiful day and I had a good feeling everything was going to be just fine.

OVER TIME NIGERIA has become plagued by transnational human trafficking which has become a major source of profit and destination in Africa. Though the government and local authorities work to stop the trafficking, the problem largely remains unchecked. Many ports go unmonitored allowing traffickers to pass through security checkpoints undetected, taking their victims to different locations around the world. Human trafficking is a lucrative business and it is quite easy for those involved to slip under the radar as well as avoid prosecution.

Traffickers prey on victims desperate to leave abusive circumstances and escape dire economic conditions. They may be facing an abusive family member and, once backed into a corner, will do anything to get themselves out. The person may also be struggling with making money and paying bills. Faced with the struggle to find good-paying jobs, the thought of a better life is enticing to them.

Victims are promised jobs, education, opportunities, large sums of money, and hopes of a bright future and greater life in another location away from home. It seems too good to be true, and it is. Once the victim agrees to relocate, they are trafficked to a new location; it's only when they arrive at their destination that they realize they've been tricked.

They are then told the truth of the situation. The victims become afraid, wanting to go back home but are threatened into cooperation. This terror-enforced "cooperation" is one of the many reasons this crime goes unrealized and unpunished. If the victim does not speak up or those around the victim do not recognize the signs of a human trafficking crime, then it appears all too easily that the victim is going willingly. They are trapped and forced to become human slaves and free laborers for a Madam with no visible way out.

Back then, I knew about the mistreatment of these people, but I did not realize how close it was to me until I heard about a girl named Farida who was experiencing it firsthand. I had been hearing about Farida's very unfortunate situation for months. In conversation with my sister, she would casually mention a story about a young girl from Nigeria who was being mistreated by a lady in the United States. Those stories would haunt my dreams, the face of a fearful young girl always present.

Farida was captured because of the promise of a modeling opportunity in Libya. This opportunity was introduced to Farida by Didi, someone she had met through her aunty. She never suspected that Didi would try to harm her or exploit her dreams. She frequently told her about how wonderful the opportunity was and the financial independence it provided. This enticed Farida because she had been looking for work and was unable to find any because she was unable to read or write. She desperately wanted a way out of her depressed economic situation and the chance to help her family. She had three younger sisters and wanted to provide a good life for them. At the same time, she sought a new, more exciting world of promise and opportunity. She had a deep desire to make something of herself and it was no secret she wanted to be a model. Farida was very beautiful and would stand in front of the bathroom mirror posing for hours. Upon hearing of the modeling job in Libya, she jumped at the opportunity. She never saw the truth coming. She had placed her trust in a person she believed had only good will toward her which ended up being her downfall.

The first red flag was the dangerous traveling conditions she endured. She and some other young women moved with armed men from Nigeria through the Sahara Desert into Libya. It was odd that these armed men needed to accompany her and some other girls to a simple modeling opportunity, but frequently the first red flag was always ignored. The next red flags were that they were not properly fed, their passports were confiscated, and the little money Farida had was taken. She was astounded by the unprofessional manner and thought she would be traveling by plane and not in a van with several other girls. Many red flags continued along the journey. The men were cruel to the women and would frequently pull the van over and maltreat them. Once they arrived in Libya, they were told they were going to be human slaves. The trafficking ring was run by Didi. Farida was chosen as Didi's personal girl, who would take care of her three children and do all the housework when they finally moved to the United States. Farida was stuck with no way out.

Didi who held Farida captive was a tough cookie. She had a worldwide human trafficking operation underway with criminal records in many countries. She employed a group of people who would do her bidding at the drop of a hat no matter how violent. Those people were loyal and worked to trap as many victims as Didi saw fit. All of this occurred under the nose of the governing bodies of each country. Not enough was done to stop her from doing what she wanted.

Didi oversaw pimps who went out to find victims for her and help build her empire. Following customary practices, they would promise the girls education, jobs, opportunities, and a better life. Once the girls made it to the promised location, they would sadly discover they had been tricked and were held captive. By the time they realized what had happened, it was too late. The girls' needs and desires were exploited.

She also had other young women with Farida and they were all referred to as "the girls." Those girls would follow her orders for fear of being beaten or their families hurt. She was a mean and stern lady who showed no mercy to her girls. She kept a whip on her at all times for intimidation and ran her camp with an iron fist. If she saw fit, she would beat them into compliance.

She wanted to make it known that she was the boss of everyone and made all of the decisions for everything. She was greedy and power-hungry with the not so good looks to match. She was a grimy woman who was short and stocky. She wore bright red and blue hair, long nails, and a large beer belly. The sight of her would turn anyone's appetite.

She ordered beatings and humiliations. She made sure the girls never had a moment to themselves and never got any rest nor sleep. There were many girls in and out of her home all the time. They cycled through like toys on a conveyor belt. If a girl was never seen again, the others were told they escaped. No one knew if that was true or not. One girl would leave and a new girl would take her place instantly. The cruelty was unmeasurable and the loneliness hit the girls heavily. There was no chance for friendships, they were there to work.

They were beaten and humiliated in every way possible. They had to be obedient in the face of violence and horrible inhumane treatment. They were threatened to be locked up if they did not comply and some witnessed others being locked up for days. They were given a quota of money they are required to make each day to pay back for travel expenses and food, which would be more than average. If the quota was not met, there were harsh consequences. There was no kindness shown towards the girls whatsoever. It was hell on earth.

Women are not the only victims of human trafficking, young boys are abducted and forced to become street vendors and perform free labor. They are nothing more than machines to those in charge.

If the young victims are lucky enough to be found and saved from their terrible lives, they may never see justice. Rescued survivors are sometimes quiet about their ordeals fearing for their safety and the details are not properly provided for a successful arrest. Since many Madams have an alias, they are harder to track down allowing them to capture more victims and remain under the radar. Victims suffer physical, psychological, social, emotional, and financial impacts following their ordeals. Upon their return, many victims are shunned for not having any financial means, resulting in anxiety, depression, insomnia, and medical issues. Nigeria has rehabilitation programs in place to assist victims in integrating back into society consisting of shelter, education, and medical care.

Now I know that all of this could so easily be missed because those involved are quiet and forced into submission. In Farida's case, Madam Didi was very powerful. She was someone you could not mess with.

You might never expect to have interaction with those who exploit these young women or the women themselves, but the people involved in this tragic crime ring are all around you.

I learned that Didi, now in the United States, was friends with a woman named Lulu, who was also friends with my sister. Lulu would call my sister to tell her of the events as they were taking place each day. My sister would in turn tell me of the events going on with Farida. Anytime I spoke to my sister, there was a new story of another incident of Farida's maltreatment, the horrors of which stuck with me each day.

Some of the stories were inhumane, disturbing, terrifying, and very hard to listen to. Farida worked tirelessly without pay. She was a slave to Didi and had to be there to attend to whoever she wanted her to serve in whatever capacity. She was a free nanny to Didi's three children and other children who came to visit. The forced labor would exhaust her, but Farida would find no rest or nourishment. She was only allowed to eat food that was fit for the trash. Once Didi and her entourage ate, Farida was given the scraps. The scraps were never enough to fully nourish her and sometimes the food was so bad when received, that she did not eat at all.

At night, Farida's body was being bitten and she was not allowed to sleep. Most nights, tired from being overworked during the day, while trying to get some sleep, she would be woken up and put back to work again. Didi was so wicked, that she made Farida sleep on the bare floor by the closet in the corridor. All the five bedrooms in her house had comfortable beds and two bedrooms were not slept in.

In the mornings, after what little sleep she might have had, Farida was responsible for getting the children ready for the day, had to get their breakfast ready, did the cleaning, the laundry, you name it, she did it. She was not sent out to run errands so she would not run away. She was not allowed to call her parents and couldn't pick up the phone whenever it rang. There were no limits to how this woman maltreated Farida.

Her parents suspected she had been trafficked when they did not hear from her since she left home. A couple of times, poor Farida tried to commit suicide. She was tired of living and was ready to end it all. After each failed attempt, she would get very little medical treatment and punishment. She was regularly starved and beaten which eventually became a part of her normal life. I would listen to the stories and I wondered why people who knew about Farida's horrible situation did nothing to help her. There were friends of Didi who visited the house, saw what was going on, and kept quiet. I found this very hard to reconcile with. It seemed like they all simply watched and didn't care. Or did they fear the repercussions of doing anything? Farida needed someone who was not afraid to do the right thing. I felt after hearing of her maltreatment day after day that someone needed to do something. As I watched not a single person lift a finger to help her, I decided that that person would have to be me. I also knew that I needed a way in, someone on the inside to aid me or I'd never be able to help Farida.

Lulu and Didi were very close. They became best friends in childhood. Over time, after the trust was built, Didi started to display her questionable criminal maltreatment of Farida to Lulu. She couldn't conceal her style of wickedness from her inner circle any longer. I later learned that as time went on, Lulu verbally disagreed with her best friend about the way she was treating Farida. I began to believe that to help Farida, I would need someone who knew quite a lot about Farida and Didi. I felt the person who would aid me would have to be Lulu, the one who always called my sister to complain about what Farida was going through. I knew that if I could sway her, I could get one step closer to saving Farida.

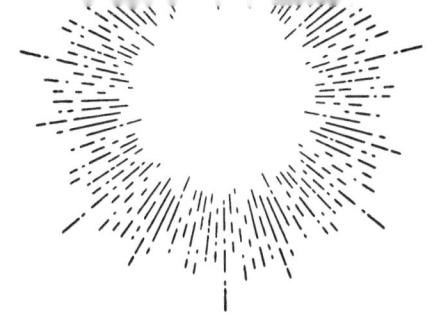

CHAPTER SIX:
FREEING FARIDA

*Lulu disagreed with her best friend about the
way she was treating Farida. Because of her
disagreement, she gave her assistance when I told
her I wanted to take Farida away from there.*

MY OFFICE WAS my haven. I decorated my place as
beautifully as I did my apartment in London. In my
lovely office, I had a shiny black mahogany desk with a
huge comfortable leather chair. The chair reminded me
of a Queen's royal chair because of how big, fluffy, and
extravagant it stood. On my desk were a medium-sized
golden globe, a calendar, a beautiful wall clock gifted to
me by my parents on my last birthday, and a statement
cup for my pens and pencils that read, "Prayer changes

everything". I took pride in keeping my office area clean and organized. On the left side was a full library filled with all the books I had collected over the years, written by my favorite authors. I also had different versions of the Holy Bible - I love to read the Bible. The right side was where I did yoga, meditated, prayed, and completed my spiritual devotion for the day. This was designed as a peaceful area filled with decorative pillows, heavily scented candles, and a lot of religious books. Close to my windows were the many plants I nurtured each day by watering and watching them thrive while at the same time appreciating nature and its beauty. I had several plants of all shapes and sizes. I had a patio door attached to the office where I could go outside, look around me, and marvel at the awesomeness of the Almighty. I loved the peaceful feeling I always had, looking out of my window or standing on my patio, enjoying the beauty of the earth. When I was in my office, nothing else mattered and when the door was closed, I was not to be disturbed. It was my own space. There was bliss!

Looking up at the sky is always a calming and spiritual experience for me. I immediately feel the presence of my

Creator whenever I turn my gaze towards the sky. Each time I do this, the first two verses of the one hundred and twenty-first Psalm come to my mind, "I will lift up my eyes unto the hills, from whence comes my help. My help comes from the Lord, who made heaven and earth". (NKJV).

On this particular day, I was standing on my patio, looking up and marveling at how beautiful the clouds were. They looked like a collection of beautiful light blue and white cotton wool, dancing gracefully in the sky with the sun peeking through. They were so fluffy that it looked as though you could bounce on them. The surroundings were so quiet with only the birds gladly chirping, jumping from one tree to another, simply having a great time, undisturbed. They were a beauty to watch and the sound they made was so melodious. I laid my head back in my chair and closed my eyes to take in the moment, taking a deep breath.

Out of nowhere, I heard a voice in my head telepathically say, "Go and take her away from where she is being abused."

It startled me at first and I had to gain my bearings to truly grasp the message given to me by this distinct voice. The voice must have known I did not immediately pick up on the message, so it repeated more sternly but still clearly, "Go and take her away from where she is being abused."

This was my chance, I thought. I had wondered several times about how Farida could be helped, if not by people who knew her but by me. The problem was how to go about it. With this message, I knew there would be a way. And there was!

The message was so clear that I had to take action quickly. I knew exactly what and whom the voice was referring to. The voice was referring to Farida. I heard the voice and knew I had to rescue her from where she was being abused. I immediately began to construct a plan of action.

Where do I start? How am I going to do this? I did not know her. I did not know her abuser. I did not know where they lived, or any pertinent details needed to successfully rescue her. The only information I had was what I was being told by Tayo, my sister, who was listening to stories from Lulu. Tayo was passing the information as she heard it. I wasn't sure how many of the details were actually correct because the information was given to me in the form of, "I heard this and I heard that." Nonetheless, without hesitation, I made the decision to do what the voice ordered me to do. I was ordered to rescue Farida. I picked up the phone, called Tayo, and told her I was going to rescue Farida. I knew I had to be blunt and direct so she would know I was serious. This was not going to be an easy conversation because she would think I was about to do the most stupid thing ever. Knowing her kind heart, she would have helped Farida if it was an easy task to do, but she had no clue how she could go up against Didi and her madness. Understandably, Tayo was concerned for her safety and the safety of everyone she held dear.

After a few rings, Tayo answered the phone in her usual happy morning voice. I got right to the point telling her I was going to free Farida. She was very surprised when I told her what the voice advised me to do. She begged me not to get involved. Her next question was to ask me why I wanted to get involved in anything this dangerous. She went through her whole spill of how I needed to stay out of it. What if Didi found out it was me? Our family could be in severe danger. She wondered how I was going to succeed in rescuing Farida without getting into trouble and being harmed. She did not hold back in telling me how unreasonable I was for considering this. Even though

I didn't need her permission to go ahead, I knew I couldn't do anything without her help. I would have to convince her to understand why she had to support me. I needed her to understand my stance.

I waited for her to calm down and I told her, "Well, I heard the voice loud and clear telling me to free Farida. I have to do it anyway and I am not afraid. Are you going to help me or not?"

I suddenly realized I was not afraid. A warm tingle went down my spine as I had the realization that the Lord would take care of me during this mission. Sensing my devotion to the voice I heard, reluctantly, my sister advised me to call Lulu because she did not personally know Farida. Lulu would have more information about Farida and how to help rescue her. She finally gave me Lulu's phone number. I was thankful to her for understanding and providing me with the information to point me in the right direction. I promised her I would be careful and I proceeded with my mission of Freeing Farida.

I took a deep breath and called Lulu. I was not expecting the deep and raspy voice I heard when she answered the phone. I introduced myself and explained to her that I was going to Didi's house to free Farida from bondage. Furthermore, I explained I had been hearing of how awful Farida was being treated and I needed her to help me free her. I did my best to sound confident so she would be more inclined to provide me with the information I needed. I told her it was imperative I rescued Farida as soon as possible. She also wondered how I was going to do that. Lulu informed me that Didi kept a pretty tight hold on Farida and would not let her go without a fight. Farida was very useful to her and would not find life easy if her slave wasn't a part of it. Lulu asked if I would have someone with me to protect me and I said, "Yes, my Father in heaven."

She was quiet for a moment. When she spoke, I could tell by her shaky voice that she was afraid for my safety. I told her the Lord would show me the way and that I was not afraid. After sensing my conviction, She let me know Didi was not going to be home that day because her sister was having a birthday party far away from her house. Lulu was Didi's best friend and knew her movements on a daily basis. I was happy to hear of the upcoming party because that would make it very easy for me to rescue Farida. The opportunity had been unleashed through divine intervention. I would not have to knock on anyone's door. It was an open house party. She revealed to me she would be there also and agreed to help me. I was elated. I was very grateful. I immediately asked for the address of the event and she willingly gave it to me.

After I got the information I needed, I must have thanked her a hundred times. I was still telling her how grateful I was after she had dropped the phone. When I realized she had hung up, I got up, going directly into action. I jumped up, took a quick shower, and frantically packed a bag. It was going to be a long ride and I needed supplies for the rescue. I packed a blanket, and a hat and made sure I had money. Happily, humming a song, I jumped in my car. I was so excited. My adrenaline was pumping full force and I did not have time to think about anything but to get to the party where Farida was. I thought of asking my friend's son to go with me but changed my mind because it would take me in the opposite direction to pick him up. I was physically going all alone on this mission. Spiritually, I had the Lord with me. I realized He was all I needed. It never occurred to me that Farida might not want to leave with me, a complete stranger, who showed up to take her to an unknown destination. Determined and undeterred, I proceeded with the rescue and shoved all doubts to the back of my mind. It was a cold day and the sun was shining brightly to light my way. It was as if the sun was my constant companion, following me, guiding my car up the highway to the address I had been given. It was a beautiful day and I had a good feeling everything was going to be just fine. I drove in silence and intuitively felt the voice with me, assuring me that everything would go well. As I drove to the party, I prayed and asked the Lord for guidance and discernment. This was a one-woman purpose.

I drove to the house in my army green Acura Legend. Not giving myself away, I surveyed the location. It was a luxurious neighborhood on the wealthy side of Suwanee Georgia. Expensive cars lined the driveways with huge houses adorned with well-manicured lawns and waterfalls in front. Children were riding their bikes up and down the street having a good time. I drove around the block a few times after locating the house. Men and women were standing outside the house talking, drinking, and smoking cigarettes. Many cars lined the streets for miles. It was a huge three-story white house with red paint on the window sills and shudders. There was a big red wooden door at the front entrance with a big gold handle. There was a long driveway wrapping to the house from the street. It seemed to be the party of the year with loud music and lots of partygoers. Everyone appeared to be having a good time. Driving around, I decided to slow down when I got to the front of the house. Making sure no one noticed me through my slightly tinted window on the driver's side, I looked through the huge window of the house and saw the party with people dancing, eating, and conversing. I tried to look for Farida and did not see anyone that looked like a slave. I did not want anyone to notice me, so I laid low in my seat. I had a hat over my eyes. I was glad I got the muffler of my car fixed a few weeks ago. This made the car exceptionally quiet. I needed to leave the engine on to heat up the car. As I waited, I was happy with the knowledge that GOD was on my side, working in my favor.

I called Lulu.

Lulu came out to answer my call. She stood about six feet tall and was robust in stature. She sure had a commanding presence. She was quite fashionable with her beautiful pink frock, black stilettos, long black wig, dangling gold earrings, necklace and about twelve bangles on her right wrist. I had no idea we would be acquainted as closely as we did. When I made the first call, I was not sure what she would think of me asking her for help. The funny thing was I did not think of her potential response when I called her, it was an afterthought. I did not know if she would call me crazy or think I was crazy, I had to take the chance. I took the risk of calling her for help and she took the risk of helping me.

I told Lulu I was parked six houses away from the event place. She sounded more willing to help me now than she did earlier when we spoke. She revealed Farida had been beaten earlier in the day for refusing to eat scraps. I was glad to be here to rescue her. I was tired of hearing any more stories about this poor girl being maltreated by this wicked lady. I described my car and told her to quickly get Farida. She asked what I would do if Farida did not want to leave. I told her I was almost sure she would want to leave with me. "Please go in and get her." I begged. She told me she would call me right back and quickly hung up. Although it was a short time, it seemed like hours had passed. As I waited for Lulu's call, a group of people were walking toward my car. I bent down so they could not see me. Thankfully, they were getting a drunk person in their car and didn't realize I was there. They walked right past my car. My eyes were fixated on the white and red house and the people coming in and out. A thought entered my mind of what I would do with Farida once I had her. The whole way to the event house, I really did not have a plan as to what I would do after her rescue. Just as I started to contemplate, the phone rang.

Lulu called back to tell me Farida was busy taking care of Didi's youngest child. Farida, referred to by her madam as a slave, was being pulled in one direction after the other. Lulu got me scared when she expressed her concern that it might not be a good time to try the rescue. She felt I should try to come back some other day. She promised she would keep me posted on Didi's movements. I was livid with anger but remained calm. I would not be swayed in my decision. I had driven hours to get there and my car was packed and ready for her. I knew today was the day I had to rescue Farida. Another day and opportunity would never present itself again. Didi could get wind of me trying to rescue Farida and move her to another location. Human traffickers moved around frequently and if they moved, I would not be able to find her. Lulu might become afraid for her own safety and back out of the mission. What if she decided not to answer my calls anymore. "Today is the day," I muttered to myself.

Thinking quickly, I sternly asked Lulu to discreetly ask Farida if she was ready to leave her awful situation. We needed this important answer out of the way first. With her phone in her hand, she went back into the house. She called Farida to the side and discreetly asked if she wanted to be rescued. Farida was confused. Lulu told her there was a very nice lady waiting outside, who heard about how she was enslaved and was ready to rescue her and take her far away from Didi. I faintly heard a low young voice on the other side of the phone answer, "yes" and that she was ready to leave. She was happy and I could hear her excitement. We did not have much time left before someone would become suspicious of Lulu talking to her. I had to get her out of the house without blowing my cover.

I instructed Lulu to tell Farida to give the child she was babysitting to Didi instead of leaving her to wander around the party. Lulu and I hung up so we could get the plan in motion. Farida told Didi she had to use the restroom, Didi had no choice but to take her child while Farida discreetly made her way out of the house through the side door. It was becoming more crowded outside the house, with people scurrying around, making it impossible for anyone to notice Farida. From where I was, I could see Lulu standing outside, carefully showing Farida where my car was parked. Farida walked to the street while Lulu watched as she made her way toward me. My heart was pounding as Farida made her escape. The fear of being caught made me sweat.

As Farida anxiously ran towards my car, I came out of the car and quickly opened the back door for her to get in. I told her to lay down on the back seat and not look up. I covered her up with a blanket. She looked so small under the blanket and I could barely believe that she was there, safe, in the back seat of my car. We had completed the first part of the mission, but it was far from over. Farida still needed to be safely taken away. It was an open house and people were going up and down, in and out, no telling who could have seen her entering my car. I went back to the driver's seat and started the car while adrenaline pounded in my ears. We hurriedly drove away, leaving behind the horrible family and the monstrous woman who had ensured Farida would never rest. Driving down the road, the wheels of the car crunched against the tar, silence in the car was the soundtrack of freedom. I looked up into my rearview mirror and Lulu was gone.

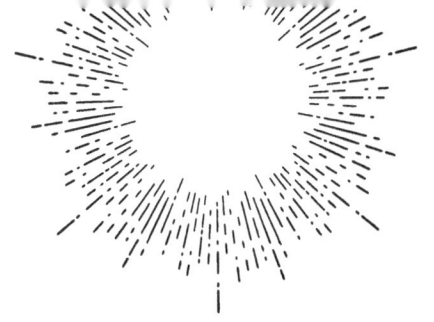

CHAPTER SEVEN:
AFTERMATH

Adiza , the young lady the madam replaced Farida
with, spoke out to authorities and told them there
was a girl before her. That girl was Farida.

CATCHING MY BREATH to calm down, after driving a couple of miles, I asked Farida if she had eaten. Lulu told me she had been beaten earlier in the day for not eating scraps and I knew she needed nourishment. It was now about six o'clock in the evening and she told me her last meal was the day before and that she was very hungry. We stopped at the nearest McDonalds and I parked far away from the building. I could not go through the drive-thru for fear of being served by someone who knew her. I wanted to be as careful as possible. I did not want to rescue Farida and then lose her because of my negligence.

As we circled around for a parking space, Farida told me she had never eaten McDonald's before. "I'll get you something you'll enjoy, just hide in the car and I'll be right back." I told her. I got out and hurried inside. Luckily the wait wasn't long as there was only one person in line with a child. I used my discretion and ordered her the ten-piece Chicken McNuggets meal, picking coke as her beverage. As I brought the food to her, she sat up, smiled at me and thanked me with a soft innocent voice. We were seeing each other face to face for the first time. My heart instantly went out to her. I knew I had to protect her and make her trust me. I sensed she would be special to me from that day forward and vice versa. She looked very thin, dehydrated and extremely malnourished. Her skin was scaly and she had pimples all over her face. Her hair was unkempt and very dry. Underneath her big brown eyes were dark circles that I believed she got from not getting enough sleep. She looked worn out and extremely tired. I instantly became more protective of her and wanted to keep her safe. I watched her from the mirror as she hungrily devoured her food. Watching her made me so sad, it brought hot tears down my cheeks. She fell asleep as soon as she finished eating her meal. I felt sorry for her, wondering when was the last time she had a restful time. I was happy for her. With the radio on, playing nice music of yesteryears that I always enjoyed listening to, I happily drove straight to my house, where she stayed, until I was able to figure out the next step for her future.

Farida and I became mother and daughter. She was a beautiful addition to our small family. She and my daughters became friends and hung out together. They treated her like their sister and we were all very happy with this beautiful young lady who felt she belonged with us. And she really did for a while. It was time to help Farida make a life for herself now that she had been rescued. Because of her status, the only job she could do was to take care of children like she had done before. That prompted me to ask around, outside where we lived, for someone who needed a nanny for young children. For obvious reasons, she had to go very far away. After several months of hiding at my house, the Lord answered our prayers. We found her not only a job, but a very happy home where she got all the love she craved and deserved.

My sister got in touch with our cousin, a nurse who lived in Baltimore, five hundred miles away and needed someone to take care of her two children while she worked at night. I told Farida about having to move to another State and make some money. That was the reason she left home with Didi in the first place. It was not easy convincing her to take the job because her past experience still lingered on in her memory. She cried and cried and cried. She was scared and I understood how she felt. She trusted no one else but me. "I cannot keep you here forever and you have a beautiful future ahead of you." I told her.

I knew I couldn't help her any further as I didn't have much more to offer. I had completed my task of rescuing her and I was at peace. She would have gone back to her family, but madam had confiscated her passport. I called Lulu, updated her on our next move, and asked if she could drive Farida to Baltimore. Apart from not having an identification to board the airplane, I also could not risk putting her on any other public transportation for fear of being recognized by other travelers who could know her.

Lulu willingly agreed to make the long trip in a rental car, another form of disguise.

She arrived safely in her new home, met her new family and felt safe and happy. She was able to get proper medical attention and continued her road to recovery. She was paid a salary, more than she expected and had enough money to take care of herself, her parents and siblings at home. Farida was free, she was safe again. She called many times to thank me and to tell me how happy she was. I was and still very grateful to my Creator for using me in FREEING FARIDA. He gave me a mission that was beautifully accomplished by giving me all the provision I needed.

Lulu had to stay away from Didi because she was suspected of having a hand in Farida's disappearance. A few people had seen her and Farida together and saw her go in as soon as the army-green Acura Legend drove off. Didi was informed and the threats started. Lulu had planned to relocate back to Nigeria before Farida's rescue. She had applied for a particular job and was lucky to have been called for an interview. This was a very good job that would earn her a lot of money. She had to go!

She had to leave her handsome boys Nat and Dave behind for about a month because of school. She called to let me know she had to go to Nigeria and would be away for some time. We routinely kept in touch after the rescue events subsided. We became friends. She was aware her friend believed she was instrumental to Farida's disappearance and that she and another unknown person had helped Farida escape. Didi, still very angry with Lulu, told their common friends how she would retaliate and make Lulu pay for betraying her. She now saw Lulu as an enemy and she was going to deal with her, showing no mercy.

Didi's family lived in Nigeria and Lulu knew she could be in danger when she got back home. She was going to keep her whereabouts and travel activities known to a few trusted individuals. She would also need someone with her to protect her everywhere she went. After informing me she'd be going back home for the interview, I had questions for her. She was there for me, it was my turn to be there for her. "Every good turn deserves another" my mother used to tell us when we were young. I knew she would need help with Nat and Dave. Whatever she needed me to do for her, I would willingly do with joy.

"Are the children going with you?" I asked.

She told me the children would only move back with her after the job was secured. Also, she did not feel comfortable taking them to Nigeria unless it would be safe to do so, nor would she blindly take them there to struggle with her.

Life could be very tough for a single parent just beginning to settle down in a country where it is the norm for people to struggle to survive. She would be gone for four weeks, maybe more depending on how the whole situation turned out.

"I am expecting to be gone for about four weeks. It could be more depending on what happens with the job," Lulu said.

"Who will be with the children for four weeks?" I asked.

She was thinking of getting a nanny from an agency to be with the boys during her absence and I disagreed with the decision. I didn't think a new nanny would be able to properly understand the needs of the children if left alone with them. She would not be able to get them to school, help with their homework and cook their meals the way mommy did. What if they got sick and had to go to the hospital? There was no way this arrangement would work, I told her. They were young active children who needed constant care and attention. They were active from the time they woke up until they went to sleep. This nanny having to handle children she had not met before could overwhelm her and trigger abuse. Anything could happen and we were not ready for another drama. Turning my attention back to Lulu I continued to press her about the children's schooling and daily life in her absence.

"Will they be able to attend school in your absence?"

The children went to a private school and Lulu did the school runs. She had a precise schedule for the children and she was adamant that it be followed. I had helped her to take care of the children once before and it wasn't easy. She was a hands-on mom and had given me a list of things for them to do. She had also instructed that their bedtime was at eight o'clock. Of course, I ventured away from the schedule a little and gave each child a spoonful of ice cream a little past their bedtime. She didn't find it funny and got upset with me. From the answers Lulu gave me, she did not have a great plan and as far as I was concerned she definitely would need my help. I was available and volunteered to help to take care of the children while she was away. I advised her to still hire the young lady who would do all the house chores. Not only did she need someone she trusted to take care of her children almost the same way she would, but she also needed someone her children felt safe and comfortable with.

One of her neighbors would take care of the school runs and whenever he couldn't, a cab driver she used regularly would be available. The cab driver was nice but not a friend of the family. He seemed like a good alternative to her because she had used his service for years with no problem, but that arrangement didn't go down too well with me.

I was not going to let her leave the boys with these two people, strangers as far as I was concerned. These two decisions unnerved me.

Immediately I knew I had to step in while she was gone. I told her I'd be there for the boys and she gratefully accepted. The plan was set. I would move into her home while she was away along with the nanny to help me.

Lulu got some funny looks and heard negative comments about herself while in Nigeria. Didi's family and friends got to know Lulu had helped with Farida's escape. The main goal, therefore, was for Lulu's family and friends to protect her from being harmed.

My brother was still mad at me for the risk I took in freeing Farida when he heard how angry Didi was and about all her crazy threats. He did not mince words to let me know how upset he was with me. Telling me how disappointed he was that I risked my life for someone I did not know. He shared his distaste for me getting into someone else's business and thought I was being nosy. He feared Didi and what she could do to us. He said I put myself, my children and family members in danger. He felt I was naive and should know how people were not to be trusted. I did not share the same feelings about the situation as he did. Yes, I knew there were high risks involved but I was not afraid of anything or anyone. The more I expressed this fact to him, the angrier he got. I told him over and over again that my Father Almighty had my back and He would continue to protect me and my family, including him. I also told him I would always be my brother's keeper, no matter what. He wasn't impressed when I told him so and I didn't care how he felt. That young girl could have been any one of us, if we had not been so privileged, I told him.

I was not surprised at his reaction, we were very close and he had always been my protector. He acted more like my father than my older brother. When he heard I would be staying at Lulu's while she was away, he got worried and said I was crazy. He said I was carelessly exposing myself to danger by being involved with Lulu. Listening to stories about how desperate madam was to deal with Lulu gave him ammunition to continue his rants of how poor my decision-making skills were. I got irritated and stopped arguing with him. I started ignoring his comments and would not say a word. After a while, he let me be and we decided to agree to disagree.

Lulu got the job. She came back to pack all of their belongings and finally moved back home. She arranged for the children to go to a boarding school. With tears in her eyes, she told me she was moving back with mixed feelings. I prayed with her and told her all would be well. She knew her friend was not happy with her. I called Lulu regularly reminding her she needed to continue to pray and believe all would be fine. When the school year ended, instead of asking the children to come to be with her, she decided to send them to London to stay with her cousin until it was safe for them to join her. She was receiving threatening phone calls and notes were being delivered to her doorstep every day. It seemed to have gone on for eternity. People called Lulu's family regularly during the day and at night threatening them. They were followed as they carried on their everyday activities. They would be running normal everyday errands, look up in the rearview mirror and a car would be following them all the way to their next destination. When they parked, the car took off. She was threatened to be dealt with and nothing would be done about it. People got away with murder in a country like ours and they still do, every single day. Lulu was thrown into a cycle of hell, thanks to her once-upon-a-time best friend and her anonymous entourage.

When the children eventually left London and went to be with their mother, they had to be homeschooled because the threats were endless. Lulu had to move several times, making life very unstable for her, Nat and Dave. I knew Lulu regretted getting involved in helping to free Farida even though she never told me so. I stayed in touch and helped in any way I could. Several times, strangers went to Lulu's house, asking her security guard if they could see her. Each time they went, Lulu would be hiding at her friend's house a few minutes away. Her family could not visit her because it was unknown if they would follow their car to her current hideout location. Lulu moved from place to place and never stayed at one location too long. Sometimes I felt guilty and sad for getting this family into this mess but most times, I would tell myself that we did what we had to do and everything would be alright soon. I was hopeful.

It was rumored that Didi had fled the country because the authorities were after her for human trafficking and child abuse. An investigation was in full swing. She abandoned her beautiful five bedroom home, four cars, her part time well-paying job for fear of being arrested and jailed, like Moses in the Bible after killing the Egyptian. After a while, Didi fled from one place to another believing Lulu was after her the way she was after Lulu and her family.

Several years later, Didi decided to sneak into the United States forgetting she was wanted dead or alive. She was coming in through an airport she believed would be safe. How wrong could she be? She got arrested and taken into custody. That began a phase of her life she never believed could happen. It was time to pay for everything she had done to make other people's lives miserable. "Love your neighbor as yourself," the Bible says, a commandment many people find very hard to follow - Didi was definitely one of such people. It was payback time, not by Farida, but by the authorities who were ready to fight not only for Farida, but for everyone she had trafficked and abused. She was in for a hard time and knowing this, she had to tell lies after lies to defend herself while in custody and investigations ensued.

Farida had to come back to Atlanta for the investigations. Adiza, the young lady who replaced Farida was summoned for questioning. Adiza was a very smart young lady. She didn't only tell her tales of woe, she supported her stories with pictures of her swollen lips, scared face, black eye and marks of being beaten all over her body. Unlike Farida, who had no pictures to show, she had all these exhibits to back up her stories.

At a press conference where I had to face about seventy police officers, I was bombarded with numerous questions. One officer asked me "Why did you not report the incident to the authorities?" I simply told him, "I was only interested in saving a child in danger who had tried to take her own life and not interested in getting anyone into trouble." They asked me if I would risk doing that again and my answer was a big YES!!! I would do it over and over and over again. I got a standing ovation and several minutes of applause. It felt good. I was proud of myself. I was used in Freeing Farida the innocent girl that could have been no more if I had not listened to that vivid soft voice I heard those years ago.

She later told me that when the dust settled, she would love to become a human trafficking advocate working with human rights organizations and governments around the world. She would love to speak at conferences and share experiences. She also believed that her purpose in life was to help other victims in "FARIDA'S" situation. She would provide women and girls who were rescued from a human trafficking situation get the additional resources needed to successfully enter back into society.

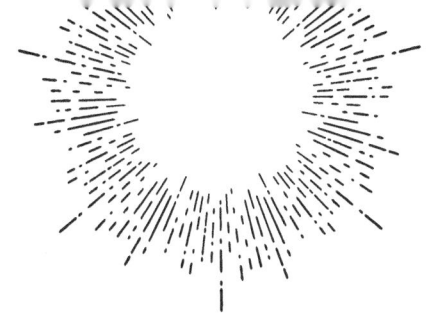

CHAPTER EIGHT:
FREEDOM

She was telling the people at the door her mother was inside, referring to me as her mother. She had grown accustomed to calling me, mommy.

THE FIRST YEAR after I rescued Farida, she was still with me. I had become like her second mom and still wanted to protect her. I didn't need to keep her for as long as I did but I did anyway. All through the year, nothing dramatic happened and we settled into normal everyday life. I could not help her even though I wanted to. She could neither read nor write proper sentences in English. Neither was she legally adopted by me as she was already an adult when I rescued her. I would not be able to answer questions if any had to be asked. Additionally, it would be dangerous to keep her with me because Didi lived in Atlanta.

After a while, Lulu moved back to Atlanta with the boys. And unknown to me while Farida was in Maryland an investigation was going on. During the investigation, Farida was found and had to come back to Atlanta. She had many questions to answer and so many stories of her traumatic experience to share. Every horrible experience she had tried to put behind her had to be reported to help her case. It was very sad and extremely difficult for her to do this, but she had to do it anyway. Investigations continued and I was later discovered at Lulu's house to tell my own side of the story.

I was not aware when Farida moved back to Atlanta. We briefly lost touch but she stayed on my mind. I knew she was okay and living her best life with a family that loved and appreciated her. I did not find out about her return until two years later when I turned fifty-five. Not knowing what I was getting myself into, I had decided not to buy gifts for my guests. I wanted to be creative and make my own gift of mixed spices as party favors for everyone to take home with them. I just wanted something different from the regular takeaway gifts. In excitement, creative me happily mixed eleven different spices together. I started putting them in the containers and midway through the exercise, I suddenly became tired. My hands ached, my back hurt and I started to sneeze as the mixture started going into my nostrils. I wanted to give up but how could I, after spending so much money on the spices and the containers. I still had several containers to fill and labels to stick on the bottles. I was upset, sick, and overwhelmed. It then dawned on me to ask for help. The first person that came to my mind was Lulu. I called her, and told her what I was going through and that I needed her to come over and help me. She gave me the best birthday gift on the phone when she told me Farida was in town and that she would bring her over. That was a birthday surprise!

I screamed, "Farida is where?"

She said, "Farida is here, in Atlanta."

I immediately asked, "Why and when did she come back here?"

She told me, "Farida had to come back because of what was going on with the investigations." All of which I was not aware of at the time.

Lulu arrived at my home with Farida. She looked so different from the Farida that left a couple of years ago. She was beautiful. She was confident. She was happy. We hugged and we were so excited to see each other. She told me she had been trying to reach me but I had changed my number. That was an excuse though and I brushed it aside because it didn't really matter. I was too happy to see how great she looked and how happy she was. She was doing very well, my prayer for her had been answered. We chatted for hours while we worked. There was so much to catch up on. I was so excited to see her that I forgot about the discomfort I was feeling before she arrived. It was a beautiful day. It was a wonderful reunion. We spent the whole day together talking about everything.

Lulu had to go out of town and asked me to move in and help take care of Nat and Dave, with Farida there to help. Farida was now living with Lulu without any fear of being harmed because Didi had fled the country. Farida rode with me every day to take the children to and from school. We were getting into a routine that had become so familiar to me. I had stayed with them a couple of times in the past.

One fine morning after we had dropped off the children in school, I was in the kitchen making breakfast when the doorbell rang. I told Farida to get the door. As she was heading for the door, she asked me if I was expecting anyone. I was not expecting anyone and I wondered who it could be. It was too early for parcel deliveries, the gardener had come to mow the lawn two days before, and we had not ordered any groceries to be delivered. Farida had no friends who would come to see her so early in the morning and no one in Atlanta knew I was at Lulu's. My children knew but they were both in Florida. I was not expecting anyone. Who could be ringing the doorbell so early in the morning? I became curious.

Farida went to get the door and a man and a woman walked in both in FBI uniforms. I nearly had a fit. What could they be doing here? I wondered. Farida on the other hand was smiling and happy to see them. She felt comfortable around them while my head was busy asking a hundred and one questions that had no answers. They greeted Farida warmly and familiarly, asking her how she had been.

"Hello, my friends. How are you doing today?" I heard Farida's voice. "My mom is here."

I got a little confused and thought she was telling them her biological mother was with her. "Is she going nuts?" I asked myself. The only people at the other end of the room were two white people in FBI uniforms. It then occurred to me that she was actually referring to me when I heard the word "mom." She had grown accustomed to calling me, mommy. The officers and I exchanged greetings while I was still wondering in my head what they could be doing here. They told me they had tried to reach me several times but could not with the number Farida had given them. Lulu on the other hand did not tell me about the investigation and didn't give them my number either, telling them she didn't have my current phone number. I think she was trying to protect me. I was not aware the FBI had been involved. They came into the house, looked at me, and asked if I was Farida's real mom. I told them I was not her biological mother but the mother who released her from bondage. Farida proudly emphasized that I was the one that came to take her away from "that wicked woman" referring to Didi.

"We have questions for you. Please sit down," the lady said.

They truly had questions for me. I knew I didn't do anything wrong but I was sweating from my head down to my toes and it was cool inside the house!

They interviewed me and recorded every single word that came out of my mouth. It was recorded when I sneezed. It was quite tiring and overwhelming. I didn't enjoy the exercise at all.

I was asked questions like "why did you rescue Farida? What pushed you to do it? Did you know Farida prior to this? Did you know her Boss?"

I answered all the questions, still sweating. Farida had been with this lady who had many friends. They could have done something. They could have tried to free this innocent young girl from the grip of this tough lady but they didn't. I was sent to rescue Farida and I did. I listened to her story for months from my sister who was living in another state. I heard of a young girl who was trying to kill herself because she was being abused. Had I been listening to the story and done nothing, and she took her life, I would also have contributed to her suicide. That was the way I saw it. I told them.

By the time I was being interviewed, Didi was still in Nigeria. They asked me if I knew where she was, I told them I had never set my eyes on her. I did not know her, nor did I know anything about her. They asked if I knew anyone that knew her. I told her I only knew Lulu who was the biggest help in Freeing Farida. I told them I knew nothing about Didi and I felt like telling them to leave me alone. They asked me so many questions. They repeated the same question several times. Perhaps they thought I would give different answers to the same question. They wanted to be sure I was telling the truth I guess. I was disgusted and got frustrated. The court case did not begin until three years after Madam was arrested. Farida's and Adiza's parents and everyone who was involved had to be present in court throughout the duration of the case that lasted for a long time. Justice was on Farida's side. She was so happy and cried for joy. Farida was free!

The state government got Farida an apartment and work permit to enable her to get a job and take care of herself. I attended the press conference where I was bombarded with questions by many police officers and other law enforcement agencies. I went for interviews a few times at the Georgia Bureau of Investigation. Farida's case was featured on CNN with all names withheld to protect us. I was a guest speaker at a religious television station in Atlanta where we discussed different ways to help victims of abuse. I sat with the abused and their parents. It was one of the saddest days of my life.

There was a couple who lost their daughter because she was abused by her live-in boyfriend. By the time they knew, it was too late to help her. He's now serving a jail term. Sitting in the same room, listening to the parents and victims of abuse and human trafficking broke my heart. I was strong enough to hold back the tears while we were live, but after the program I got to talk with some of the parents and I could not hold back the tears. They flowed uncontrollably. It was difficult to listen to the pitiful and emotional stories they were sharing. As Farida's story got more exposure, it appeared on other TV stations and I was invited to speak. However, I only went to one TV station. Apart from being shy on camera, I thought I had done enough at that particular time. All I wanted to do was to save someone's life. I didn't want any fame and I also didn't want to expose myself as I had myself and my family to protect. The whole event went on from 2003 to 2011.

The day I testified in court was when Didi and I saw each other face to face for the first time. She was right to have suspected her dear friend Lulu was involved in FREEING

FARIDA because she really was, but that day she knew someone else whom she had never met before was also involved - ME.

Testifying was not easy for me to do but I had to do it anyway. I was nervous because I had to speak in public, something I was not used to. I was also nervous because appearing in court brought about mixed feelings that I didn't expect. I drew strength from above and stood my ground, facing the woman who had imprisoned Farida. At the same time, I felt sorry for Didi especially when I saw how miserable and scared she looked, perhaps wondering who I was and what I had to say. It hurt to testify because I knew everything I had to say on that day would be used against her. It was time for her to face her punishment. I was happy for Farida. Didi got the judgment she deserved. She was free and so was I.

During the trial, it was obvious Farida was in pain. She was quite emotional. Coming face to face with Didi for the first time after several years was very difficult for her. Everything she was struggling to forget came flashing back. She broke down uncontrollably several times, crying like a child in excruciating pain. There were moments when I had to embrace her and wipe her tears during coffee breaks. Farida remained strong after the trial. Her pain wouldn't be healed with the conclusion of the trial, but she would definitely heal with time. She had professional counseling for quite a while because she went through so much for too long. Support from family and friends who showered her with so much love made healing faster than expected.

In the end, justice was served. Didi was convicted of abuse and human trafficking and and was sentenced to several years in prison.

Farida, Lulu, Adiza and many others involved could finally know the peace and safety that Didi had denied them for so long.

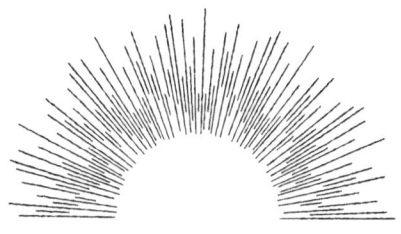

EPILOGUE

TODAY, THE WORLD continues to turn, and, by the grace of GOD, our story has a happy ending. Lulu is doing just fine. She lives in Atlanta with her two handsome boys, now young men. Farida gets more and more beautiful with age and now lives in an upscale part of Georgia. She is doing very well, happily married to a wonderful man who showers her with so much love. They are blessed with three beautiful children. Not a day goes by that I do not think of these women and the experience we shared. How their lives had intertwined with mine and how my own world had changed with my decision to save young Farida.

I will be seventy years old the day FREEING FARIDA will launch and I'm grateful to my Creator who has given me and my family the grace to be alive and in good health.

The ups and downs of life are inevitable. I have experiences that I share regularly to help other people. I am LOVE. I am grateful to GOD who has compensated me by surrounding me with loving family and friends, beautiful children and grandchildren, natural and spiritual. They are all very dearly loved and greatly appreciated.

In the years that have passed since the rescue of Farida and the trial, I continue to use my strength to aid and advocate for those around me. Many people ask me how I was able to help a stranger so easily. The truth is I have been through several experiences like everybody else. I've seen the good, the bad and the ugly sides of life. Some experiences demand a lot of strength and whenever that is needed, I would turn to Him who created me for help. "Where the need is greatest, God's help is nearest" my beautiful sister Kemi would share with me during difficult times, quoting from The Grail Message - In The Light of Truth by Abdrushin. A lot of times, I would look back on some difficult experiences that I've had and wonder how I survived them. I survived quite a bit because my strong and loving parents birthed me. At ninety-six, my mother is still my pillar of strength. She is the one I go to for advice whenever I'm stuck. Growing up with my siblings, we saw how our parents loved and cared for other people's children. My late father had, without the permission of the parents, gone to rescue his niece who was always being battered by her husband. He got a police officer to go with him to the couple's home. My dear father packed all his niece's belongings and brought her and all she owned to our family house. He called her parents after he brought her to our home. Her parents lived in a different city so she stayed with us until her parents came to get her a couple of days later. I can proudly say of my parents that they did a beautiful job. They shaped me into the compassionate person that I am today. I cannot and will not intentionally ignore a person who needs my help. In closing, I will emphasize that the greatest strength ever is from the Almighty. Faith in Him gives me unimaginable peace, comfort, and joy.

Farida's journey should bring awareness to all - it is important to be our brother's keeper. I knew I could not change Farida's past, but I strongly believed I could and I was ready to help change her future. It is a beautiful feeling when one is able to help someone else. Find the strength within yourself and your personal experiences to be there to help those around you. In the process of helping in Freeing Farida, I also found freedom for my soul!

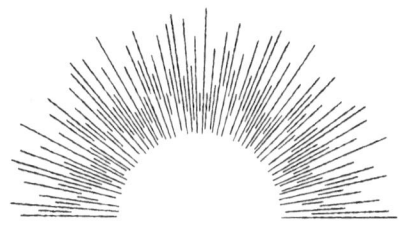

ABOUT THE AUTHOR

DOTUN IS A NATURAL when it comes to loving, nurturing, mentoring and mothering.

Teaching in London for a while after she graduated from College exposed her to children whom she interacted with in and out of school. She became a lover of children, and young adults showering them with love before she became a mother herself. It's no wonder she embarked on an exercise no one else thought of embarking on when she decided to save a young girl being trafficked - a girl she had never met before, a total stranger.

One fine morning, looking out of the window, wondering at the awesomeness of the Almighty, Dotun was sent on a mission by a voice she heard and simply could not ignore. The action she took, would change the life of young Farida forever.

Life is not a bed of roses. There are good and bad times, and Dotun has been through both. The tough times of Dotun's life, that could sometimes send her into bouts of depression did not stop her from freeing Farida from bondage. Neither did it stop her from showering live on the children and grandchildren of people she had never met.

Freeing Farida, was birthed when Dotun was going through a tough and difficult time, caring for her granddaughter during her recovery from a Bone Marrow Transplant. This procedure was done to cure her from Sickle Cell Disease.

In her book, she narrates the ups and downs of her life experiences with her 2 beautiful children, who now live in Atlanta, Georgia. Dotun currently lives with her older daughter and her lovely family, doing what she loves best.

Now 70 years old, Dotun finds absolute joy in cooking, baking, and making jewelry to sell for peanuts, but more often than not, finds herself giving them away as gifts. Giving gives her so much joy and pleasure.

She is hoping this book will be an encouragement to the right people who value the human life. It speaks of how we should not look the other way if we know of anyone being trafficked. We need to work together, and stop human trafficking.

There are numerous signs to recognize those in this situation. If you cannot get to where the victim is, speak out by reporting to the authorities. The number to call if you suspect that someone is a suspect or a perpetrator is:

080/022/7777.

In Freeing Farida, Dotun not only found joy in saving an innocent girl, she also found freedom for her soul.

CONNECT WITH THE AUTHOR:

Follow me on instagram @
freeingfarida
auntidot!

HUMAN TRAFFICKING IS a form of modern-day slavery. This crime occurs when a trafficker uses force, fraud or coercion to control another person for the purpose of engaging in commercial sex acts or soliciting labor or services against his/her will. Force, fraud, or coercion need not be present if the individual engaging in commercial sex is under 18 years of age.

If you or someone you know is in danger, call:

1 (888) 373-7888
National Human Trafficking Hotline

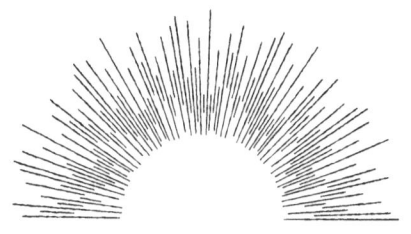

"IT IS MY GREATEST HOPE THAT THE VALUE OF HUMAN LIFE IS NEVER TO BE COMPROMISED."

Dotun Dawodu